THE UNSEEN
UNIVERSITY
CHALLENGE

Terry Pratchett's
Discworld Quizbook

THE UNSEEN UNIVERSITY CHALLENGE

Terry Pratchett's Discworld Quizbook

Compiled by David Langford

VISTA

Rearrange the following words into a well known phrase or saying:
twenty Hazel for thanks with wonderful To of years being

First published in Great Britain 1996 as a Vista paperback original
by Victor Gollancz Ltd
A member of Cassell plc
Wellington House, 125 Strand, London WC2R 0BB

© David Langford 1996
Introduction © Terry and Lyn Pratchett 1996

The right of David Langford to be identified as author of this work has
been asserted by him in accordance with the Copyright, Designs and
Patents Act, 1988.

Discworld® is a trade mark registered by Terry Pratchett

A catalogue record for this book is available from the British Library.

The Discworld Companion illustrations © Stephen Briggs 1994
Mort: A Discworld Comic illustrations © Graham Higgins 1994

ISBN 0 575 60000 4

Designed and typeset by
Fishtail Design

Printed and bound in Great Britain
by Cox & Wyman Ltd, Reading, Berks

99 98 97 96   10 9 8 7 6 5 4 3 2 1

'INTRODUCTION

by Terry Pratchett

Someone once said that the Discworld is a world and mirror of worlds.

Hang on . . . that was me, wasn't it?

But the fact is that any fantasy world is, sooner or later, our own world. It may be in heavy disguise, but it can't escape its origins. At a basic level, even the language gives it away. However towering the distant mountains, however dwarf-haunted the local woods, any character wanting to eat a piece of *zorkle* meat between two slices of bread probably has no other word for it than 'sandwich'. Every sentence the most exquisitely alien elf speaks will be filled with the echoes of Rome.

There's not a lot we can do about it. The builder of fresh worlds may well start out carefully avoiding Alsatian dogs and Toledo steel, but if he or she has any sense will one day look up from the keyboard and utter the words: 'What the hell?'

Somewhere around that point, the Discworld starts. Reality is very thin around it, you see. Influences leak across from other more prosaic worlds. A city Watchman in a breastplate and helmet and tight corner finds himself speaking in the tones of Harry Callaghan. A young druid pioneering a new type of popular music might have, for perfectly logical and defensible reasons, a name which translates as 'Bud of the Holly'.

This is all traditional stuff. A storyteller helps the narrative come alive by picking the images the readers will recognize. But there are further hidden devices. Ankh-Morpork, the main city, has Lord Vetinari as its ruler; clearly the Vetinaris have a distant relationship with the Medici. But anyone who does a tiny bit of research and some lateral thinking will work out why the city has also had, for quite a few books, noble families called the Selachii and the Venturis. There's a plot waiting there somewhere . . .

Mind you, this sort of thing rebounds. People analyse Discworld books. Some people go through the text with the thoroughness of Baconians, and write me triumphant letters about how the phrase 'Please open the window' has clearly been taken from a Czech play last performed in 1928. Others ask about the eventual fate of characters who were created at a moment's notice solely in order to be stunned by a falling mongoose. Some readers even ask what happened to characters after the end of the book.

Whence comes this desire to flesh out small worlds, to write dictionaries of Klingon, to erect signposts in fairyland? I don't know, but I'm pretty sure it's one of the activities that make us human beings instead of just some sort of advanced ape, and it probably has some kind of mysterious survival value.

I'm told the BBC has forbidden people to take Discworld as a subject on *Mastermind*, which may show unusual common sense on the part of the BBC. But at least you can now demonstrate your prowess in Discworldology in the comfort of your own home.

What more could anyone reasonably require?

Terry Pratchett

MATRICULATION

The examination papers of the wizards' college,
Unseen University, chief centre of occult learning
on Terry Pratchett's Discworld, are like no others
in the multiverse. For example, owing to wizardly
perceptions of alternate-dimensioned space, it is
necessary to caution candidates to write on no more
than three sides of the paper – or fewer than the square
root of minus one. Bilocation, clairvoyance and spells
of temporal stasis are strictly prohibited in the
examination hall.* Advanced questions in magical
theory may, if improperly tackled, reduce candidates
to small pink lizards. (This can count as a 'fail' mark.)
And so on.

Since Unseen University guards its papers closely
and our publishers mysteriously object to the
transformation of readers into lizards,** we have had
to adjust the scope of this quizbook slightly. A few
general notes and tips . . . *Please read them all before
you plunge into the book.*

* And don't think the invigilator can't see that copy of *The
Discworld Companion* in your pocket.

** Because lizards don't buy books.

¶ It would be madness or at least very, very silly to tackle the following quiz papers without a fair knowledge of Terry Pratchett's works, in particular the Discworld series, from *The Colour of Magic* (1983) to *Maskerade* (1995). New readers are warned that a few answers may reveal plot points they would rather not know prior to reading the books . . . though there shouldn't be anything quite as crude as, 'In *Men at Arms* it was the butler what done it.'

¶ It is also useful to know something about the universe in general, since one of the pleasures of Discworld is its huge range of buried jokes and sly allusions. Peter Cook's words should be an example to us all: 'I am very interested in the universe. I am specializing in the universe and all that surrounds it.'

¶ At this point we flick our fingers derisively at certain Discworld readers who have never quite grasped the fact that allusion, cross-reference, in-jokes and homage are ancient and much-appreciated literary traditions. After laboriously tracing some connection – for example, that the very name of Unseen University is a tip of the hat to the 'Invisible College' of the seventeenth-century natural scientists – these people tend to say, 'So Terry Pratchett just *stole* it?' We cannot be having with this attitude. The quiz papers which invite you to spot connections are celebrations of erudite fun, not dark hints of plagiarism. More about this in one of the Answers sections.

¶ The Archchancellor wishes it to be noted that the faculty names at the heads of the papers do not all necessarily correspond to actual Unseen courses. Some of them may be taught only in Room 3B.

¶ Candidates should not turn over both sides of the paper at once. Er, that is, you are on your honour not to turn the pages too fast, since for convenience (hunting around in the back of the book is so fiddly) each Answers section follows on from its quiz paper. Or, sometimes, next to it.

¶ Marks are awarded as indicated in the Answers sections – normally one mark per correctly answered question, but with exceptions to confuse and annoy you. You may adjust your marks retrospectively on the basis that you had it on the tip of your tongue all the time really, provided you feel a tiny bit ashamed for doing so. In particular, be generous to yourself when the answer is a minor character's name: even Terry Pratchett can't remember the names of *all* the extras on the great stage of Discworld. So, for example, 'Er, that wizard guy in *Mort*, tip of my tongue, started with C, kept sitting on pizzas, I *know* I know this one, etc. . . .' is an entirely plausible substitute for 'Igneous Cutwell'.

¶ For occasions when you're completely foxed, we have at colossal expense provided a Hints section disguised as the Faculty of Musicology quiz (page 213). This can be considered as the equivalent of using magical techniques like scrying to help do an exam paper. Unseen University reckons that anyone skilled enough in magic to do this probably deserves to pass, despite being an irritatingly clever bugger.

¶ Candidates are warned not to attempt too many questions in any given session. Overdoing it may harm the brain – leaving you to be found in the morning with a gruesomely empty skull, still clutching a book that has dribbled slightly at the binding and seems strangely ... fatter. This is a fearful cliché to be avoided at all costs.

¶ Omniscience is frowned on. (The Gods are notoriously stroppy about demarcation issues.) If you are effortlessly able to answer every single question without even checking references in Discworld books, there's likely to be something seriously wrong with the quality of your life.

Now, turn over your question papers and begin.

David Langford

Faculty of
GALLIMAUFRY

A bumper-sized mixed bag of easy questions to get
you in the mood. As the traditional formula of the
Examining Board goes,
'Thys is thine Starter for X poyntes . . . '

1   Who told a gathering of fellow-barbarians that the three
    greatest things in life are 'Hot water, good dentishtry and
    shoft lavatory paper'?

2   Which stormy insect is noted for the fractal Mandelbrot
    patterns on its wings?

3   Death's awesome flying steed that traverses the world at
    the speed of night is called . . . what?

4   Name the sacred place where the daylight was so
    particularly good for movie-making.

5   What are dwarfs most often noted for eating, aside from
    the famous dwarf bread?

6   Answer this question posed by Archchancellor Ridcully:
    'What kind of sad, hopeless person needs to write
    WIZZARD on their hat?'

7   When nocturnal mountain trolls speak of legends as being
    handed down since the sunset of time, what are they
    talking about?

7a What is the dread syllable which wizards are so cautious
    about pronouncing, and which should be avoided by any
    visitor to the temple of Bel-Shamharoth?

9 One famous climactic scene in the Discworld saga features a 50ft woman scaling Ankh-Morpork's tallest building while brandishing in one hand a terrified . . . what?

10 Who was the coven leader and headology expert who owned a hard-to-start broomstick and was the first (possibly the only) woman ever to be offered a Chair at Unseen University?

11 Which occult force opened the bronze doors of the great Temple of Om without the touch of any human hand?

12 What revolutionary new financial concept, imported by a tourist from the Counterweight Continent, caused most of Ankh-Morpork to be burned down?

13 Lady Sybil Ramkin, the celebrated swamp-dragon fancier, has as her crowning glory a mass of chestnut curls – which is notable in what way?

14 When people-eating terror comes following behind on lots of little legs . . . what material would you expect this menace to be constructed from?

15 Of which real-world musical should we be reminded by the opera title (mentioned in *Maskerade*) *Seven Dwarfs for Seven Other Dwarfs*?

16 If there was a name plaque – probably executed in tacky pokerwork – on the abode of Discworld's Gods atop Cori Celesti mountain, what would it say?

17 Which Discworld novel has two interleaved storylines that are distinguished by different typefaces?

18 Which character is famously described (and, on certain jacket paintings, perplexingly shown) as having four eyes?

19 Which trans-sane member of the Unseen University faculty is kept fleetingly stable only by doses of dried frog pills?

20 Identify the Discworld book which was advertised as follows by its American publisher: 'Who in this world, or any other for that matter, would write a novel about a football team that falls victim to a group of wily elves?'

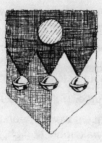

Faculty of Gallimaufry
ANSWERS

1 Cohen the Barbarian. (*The Light Fantastic*)

2 The Quantum Weather Butterfly (*Papilio tempestae*), which manipulates the 'butterfly effect' of Chaos theory to create vicious storms, generally about six inches across. (*Interesting Times*)

3 Binky. (*Mort*)

4 Holy Wood in *Moving Pictures* . . . which was very nearly titled *Hooray for Holy Wood*.

5 Rats. Preferably with ketchup: rat and ketchup costs nearly twice as much as rat alone since, well, have you ever tried rat without ketchup? (*Men at Arms*)

6 Rincewind. Of course. (*Interesting Times*)

7a The same as what we would mean by the dawn of time: trolls who awake only at night regard their 'day' as beginning at sunset. The dawn of time lies in the future. (*The Light Fantastic*)

8 'Eight.' (*The Colour of Magic*)

9 An ape – the Librarian, to be precise. Lose two marks if you said 'monkey' . . . (*Moving Pictures*)

10 Granny Weatherwax. She quite fancied one of those big wicker ones. (*Equal Rites*)

11 Hydraulics: water-powered machinery. Ultimately, in fact, the efforts of a lot of sinners pacing on the nearby Treadmill of Correction to drive a shaft and pump the water up into the system. Any answer in either of these general areas is fine. (*Small Gods*)

12 Fire insurance. (*The Colour of Magic*)

13 It is, alas, a wig. No one who has much to do with dragons keeps their own hair for long. (*Guards! Guards!*)

14 The Luggage is made from sapient pearwood, a highly magical and/or magic-resistant material. (*The Colour of Magic*)

15 *Seven Brides for Seven Brothers.* The subsidiary joke is that the sexes are unspecified because it's so extremely difficult to discover if a Discworld dwarf is male or female. For a start, they all wear beards and helmets.

16 'Dunmanifestin.' (*The Colour of Magic*)

17 *Reaper Man.* This is especially noticeable in the first hardback edition from Gollancz.

18 Twoflower, Discworld's first tourist, in *The Colour of Magic* and *The Light Fantastic.* The consensus – confirmed by his eventual reappearance in *Interesting Times* – is that this is the traditional 'four-eyes' witticism applied to a wearer of glasses, but that cover artist Josh Kirby interpreted it with inspired surrealism. Or got it wrong. One or the other.

19 The current Bursar, who has deteriorated steadily since his first appearance in *Moving Pictures.*

20 *Lords and Ladies.* Clearly it has to be, since this is the only Discworld novel with a strong elvish presence (the hero of *Soul Music* is merely an elvish impersonator). But how did publishers HarperPrism hallucinate the football team? Can this be evidence of a deep American inability to comprehend Morris dancing? Is it relevant that hardened Pratchett fans tend to refer to Americans as Merkins?* Probably not.

---

* Do not look up this word in the dictionary.

Faculty of
FIRST CAUSES

Just name the Discworld books of which these are the opening words . . .

1 This is the bright candlelit room . . .

2 The sun rose slowly, as if it wasn't sure it was worth the effort.

3 Watch . . .

4 This is the Discworld . . .

5 The wind howled.

6 There was a man and he . . .

7 The sun rose slowly, as if it wasn't sure it was worth all the effort.

8 This is a story about memory.

9 The Morris dance is common to all inhabited worlds in the multiverse.

10 This is the room where lives slip away . . .

Last reminder: don't forget the 'Faculty of Musicology' Hints section on page 213. Mark it with a slip of paper now. You may one day need it.

Faculty of First Causes
ANSWERS

1   *Mort.*

2   *The Light Fantastic: The Graphic Novel.*

3   *Moving Pictures.*

4   *Witches Abroad.*

5   *Wyrd Sisters* and, indeed, *Maskerade*. Bonus mark for naming both.

6   *Sourcery.*

7   *The Light Fantastic.*

8   *Soul Music.*

9   *Reaper Man.*

10 *Mort: A Discworld Big Comic.*

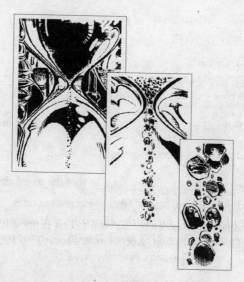

Faculty of
INVISIBLE WRITINGS

Here is a selection of extracts from various writings, engravings, inscriptions and so on, all featured within Discworld novels. Spot the context . . .

1 *Ahahahahaha! Ahahahaha! Aahahaha! BEWARE!!!!!*

2 I ATEN'T DEAD.

3 IOU 4 DOLERS.

4 We Will Not See His Like Again.

5 Stepladders Repaired.

6 Help. Help. If anyone reads this I am being held prisoner by an evil eunuch. Help.

7 *Laugh This One Off.*

8 Follow me in single file, bwanas, to fool the hated enemy.

9 Closed even for the sale of Necromancer cigarettes.

10 He said he would come but he hasn't. This is my last newt. I saved it for him. And he hasn't come.

Faculty of Invisible Writings
ANSWERS

1 One of the subtly disconcerting notes signed by 'The Opera Ghost'. (*Maskerade*)

2 Granny Weatherwax's card indicating that she's not dead but Borrowing, with her mind temporarily elsewhere in a bat, hare or whatever. (*Lords and Ladies*)

3 Promissory note magically burnt into the stone wall of an Ankh-Morpork coffee bar by Archchancellor Ridcully after his delinquent wizards had filled the place and indeed the street with coffee-smelling froth in an attempt to conjure up espresso. (*Soul Music*)

4 The wishful-thinking inscription on the pedestal of Unseen University's statue of Alberto Malich. After 2000 years of respite, alas, they did see his like again. (*Mort*)

5 From the visiting card of Giamo Casanunda, World's Second Greatest Lover ('I try harder'); also Finest Swordsman, Soldier of Fortune, Outrageous Liar . . . (*Lords and Ladies*)

6 Footnote to an Agatean tax-office directive calligraphed by Six Beneficent Winds, against his will, on the instructions of Cohen the Barbarian – who was merely *dressed* as a eunuch. (*Interesting Times*)

7 The Seriph of Al Khali's ingenious grandfather had constructed a secret tunnel full of practical jokes (automated kicks, tickles, electric shocks, buckets of whitewash, etc.). This was the inscription on the side of the final jape: an entire stone roof section, four feet thick, set to fall hilariously on the exasperated intruder. (*Sourcery*)

8   Silent-movie caption for *Shadowe of the Dessert*, subtly accounting for the fact that the army of the Klatchian desert chieftain consisted of a single camel passing the camera 100 times with varied riders. (*Moving Pictures*)

9   Irritating card once displayed on the door of the universe-traversing magic shop with the long complicated name.* (*The Light Fantastic*)

10 A particularly deviant example of the dwarf genius Hwel's discarded playscript inspirations: this speech by the 3RDE WITCHE shows the spirit of *Waiting for Godot* seeping unhelpfully into The Scottish Play.** (*Wyrd Sisters*)

* Another of its signs exhorted customers to 'Call Again Tomorrow For Spoonfetcher's Leeches, the Little Suckers'.

** Actually, the Lancre Play.

Faculty of
ANCILLARY PERSONAGES

A knowledge test about some of the Discworld's
most obscure minor characters, spear-carriers and
walk-ons . . .

1 What did Lackjaw the dwarf jeweller make for Cohen the
Barbarian?

2 Twoflower named his conjured-up dragon Ninereeds, after
whom?

3 What was Moghedron's rôle in the palace staff of Sto Lat?

4 Which beginners' course at Unseen University was taught
by Jeophal the Spry?

5 How did J.H. 'Flannelfoot' Boggis's business cards
advertise himself and his nephews?

6 For what hilarious place of imprisonment was Giggling
Lord Smince of Ankh-Morpork famed?

7 What tasty round delicacies were favoured by Norris, the
Maniac of Quirm?

8 Which country did King Mausoleum rule during the time
of the legendary war and siege involving giant wooden
livestock?

9 Prince Lasgere of Tsort wanted to become learned and
demanded that a royal road to learning be built for him
forthwith – by whom?

10 The footpad Pilgarlic and his two accomplices were
alarmed when their chosen victim escaped by doing
something very strange to a wall in the Shades . . . what?

ANSWERS

1 A set of diamond dentures. (*The Light Fantastic*)

2 His erstwhile boss Ninereeds the Masteraccount. (*The Colour of Magic*)

3 He was the palace wine butler. (*Mort*)

4 Beginners' Dematerialization. (*Equal Rites*)

5 Bespoke Thieves, 'The Old Firm'. (*Wyrd Sisters*)

6 His Laugh-a-Minute Dungeon. (*Guards! Guards!*)

7 Better known as Norris, the Eyeball-Eating Maniac of Quirm . . . (*Maskerade*)

8 Tsort. This was the Discworld version of the Trojan war. (*Eric*)

9 The philosopher Didactylos.* (*Small Gods*)

10 The intended victim – Mort, who was just beginning to get the hang of it – walked through a wall. (*Mort*)

* In our own world, Euclid was running a geometry school in Alexandria and was asked by King Ptolemy to provide an easy sound-bite version of all this hard mathematical stuff. The legendary reply was: 'Sire, there is no royal road to learning.'

Faculty of
THAUMOSELECTION

Which of the Discworld's many named wearers of robes and pointy hats did as follows . . .

1 Bequeathed his power to a child who turned out to be of the wrong sex?

2 Had a speaking brass plate screwed to the wall by his door?

3 Was briefly an expert in the breakaway oxidation phenomena of certain reactors?

4 Reckoned teleportation was straightforward, all a matter of energy absorption and attention to relative velocities?

5 Transferred his essence into his own staff?

6 Kept a small bottle of Bentinck's Very Peculiar Old Brandy in his pointy hat?

7 Gave his name to a spell that created, appropriately, a huge magical lens?

7a Invented banged grains?

9 Became, at least for a while, a zombie?

10 Devised that fearful weapon, the Wand of Utter Negativity?

11 Wrote a wizardly text called *Demonylogie Malyfycorum*?

12 After absent-mindedly drinking a bottle of potent aphrodisiac, flung himself gratefully into a freezing horse trough which soon began to emit steam?

Faculty of Thaumoselection
ANSWERS

1 Drum Billet in *Equal Rites*. His magical heir Esk was supposed to be a boy, not a girl.

2 C.V. Cheesewaller, DM (Unseen), B. Thau, B.F. – well, that's what his brass plate says aloud in *Soul Music*. 'Cheesewaller' is answer enough.

3 Rincewind, temporarily occupying another universe under the name Dr Rjinswand. (*The Colour of Magic*)

4 Ponder Stibbons. (*Interesting Times*)

5 Ipslore the Red. (*Sourcery*)

6 Mustrum Ridcully. (*Reaper Man*)

7 Fresnel. His lens spell is Fresnel's Wonderful Concentrator, recalling the stepped Fresnel lens used in earthly spotlights, headlights, etc. (*The Colour of Magic*)

7a Peavie, treasurer of the Alchemists' Guild, in *Moving Pictures*. If you object that popcorn is already known to Hwel in *Wyrd Sisters*, you may allow yourself a warm glow of pedantic satisfaction but no additional marks.

9 Windle Poons. (*Reaper Man*)

10 Ajandurah – no marks for saying Marchesa, who merely wielded the thing. (*The Colour of Magic*)

11 Henchanse thee Unsatysfactory. (*Equal Rites*)

12 Igneous Cutwell, DM (Unseen), Marster of the Infinit, Illuminartus, Wyzard to Princes, Gardian of the Sacred Portalls, If Out leave Maile with Mrs Nugent Next Door.* (*Mort*)

---

* Who, disconcerted by his visit from Mort, nervously sipped his way through a large bottle of 'Granny Weatherwax's Ramrub Invigoratore and Passion's Philtre, Onne Spoonful Onlie before bed and that Smalle'.

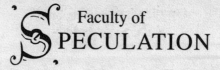

Faculty of
SPECULATION

Sometimes the linking theme of an Unseen
University paper is so transparently obvious to the
discerning that it needn't be explicitly stated.
Identify the following:

1   A celebrated philosophical treatise by Xeno of Ephebe.

2   Enthusiastic use of armour polish made this character a
    positive danger in certain situations.

3   Came to a nasty end thanks to a blue-green lump in the
    squishi, with rubbery tubes dangling from it.

4   May assist in the interpretation of sketches and designs
    by the Discworld's greatest inventor.

5   One of the four important pieces of grandmotherly advice
    that guided Desiderata Hollow through life.

6   A deadly weapon 30 feet across.

7   Used by all Assassins to avoid a certain terrible insult to
    their victims.

8   It was small and speckled, and Granny Weatherwax
    carefully buried it.

9   What Vimes was looking at when the Assassin struck
    from the Opera House roof.

10 Legendarily famous for a lightning-powered telepresence
    system.

ANSWERS

The specula in the faculty name are, of course, mirrors.

1 Xeno's book *Reflections*. (*Small Gods*)

2 Carrot's mirror-like breastplate was liable to make swamp dragons explode in the effort to swell up and outface their own images. (*Men at Arms*)

3 Nine Turning Mirrors, Vizier of the Agatean Empire. (*Mort*)

4 Leonard of Quirm, like his morphic twin Leonardo da Vinci, wrote his private notes and annotations in right-to-left reversed handwriting. Just hold it up to a mirror. (*Men at Arms*)

5 'Never get between two mirrors' – or you'll end up like, for example, Lily Weatherwax. (*Witches Abroad*)

6 The 30ft parabolic reflector on a high tower used by the Ephebians to focus the sun's rays and burn up most of the Omnian fleet.* (*Small Gods*)

7 A full-length mirror in their rooms: it would be a terrible insult to anyone if their killer were badly dressed. (*Pyramids*)

8 The one mirror in her cottage – which Lily could otherwise use to spy on her. (*Witches Abroad*)

---

*Our own Archimedes was credited with this little trick during the defence of Syracuse against Roman invaders in 212 BC. Given contemporary mirror technology, it seems unlikely. Science essayist J.B.S. Haldane suggested that maybe Archimedes never built the weapon, but that the Syracusan Ministry of Information dropped leaflets over the walls claiming he was going to . . .

9 His own face, in the cracked mirror over the basin in his lodgings. (*Men at Arms*)

10 One Sun Mirror, founder of the Agatean Empire, whose Red Terracotta Army relentlessly followed its leader's movements and commands.* Even when the leader was as inept as Rincewind. (*Interesting Times*)

*At this point we emphatically do not mention the computer game *Lemmings*.

Faculty of
ADHESIVE ULTIMATES

As is inevitable in any world where Death is a major character, plenty of Discworld's people and other entities come to sticky ends. Here is a selection of lethal agencies: name the victims.

1 A Barking Dog.

2 1000 trumpeting elephants on improvised bobsleds.

3 Anoxia in a hermetically sealed chamber.

4 Trying on the velvet cloak belonging to a ragged Queen.

5 Speaking one's own name as a route to suicide.

6 Beauty.

7 High-velocity tortoise impact.

8 Being stitched to a wall.

9 Being pushed into one's own oven by delinquent kids.

10 A red-hot poker, ten pounds of live eels, a three-mile stretch of frozen river, a butt of wine, a couple of tulip bulbs, a number of poisoned eardrops, an oyster and a large man with a mallet.

Faculty of Adhesive Ultimates
ANSWERS

1 Lord Hong and Mr Saveloy in *Interesting Times* (half a mark if you named only one, and similarly for other multiple victims below).

2 Two unnamed yetis in the Ramtop mountains. Famous last words: 'What do you get if you cross . . . a mountain with an elephant?' (*Moving Pictures*)

3 The wizard Greyhald Spold, who constructed an invulnerable refuge from Death but failed to consider 'the important part that airholes must play in an enterprise of this kind'. (*The Light Fantastic*)

4 Lettice Knibbs – lady's maid to Molly, Queen of the Ankh-Morpork Beggars. When an Assassin with a gonne is taking potshots at guild leaders, it's unwise to see how you look in the official regalia of the head beggar – as defined in the beggars' charter: 'Some in rags, and some in tags, and one in a velvet gown.' (*Men at Arms*)

5   Vincent the Invulnerable, who walked into a tough Ankh-Morpork pub and announced his chosen name aloud. (*Soul Music*)

6   A Thing from the Dungeon Dimensions: "Twas beauty killed the beast,' according to the Dean of Unseen University, but others argued that a fall from the 800ft Tower of Art might also have had something to do with it. (*Moving Pictures*)

7   Exquisitor Vorbis in *Small Gods*.

8   Unnamed opera-house seamstress* in *Maskerade*.

9   The witches' witch Black Aliss Demurrage, who is mentioned several times in the saga.

10 Murune, erstwhile King of Lancre, in *Wyrd Sisters*. He appears to have had difficulty in making friends.

---

* One of the rare occasions on which a seamstress was just a seamstress, rather than one of those naughty women at Mrs Palm's.

Faculty of
TRUE NAMES

'Why are things called what they are?' is a philosophical question fraught with uncertainty and peril. Give plausible origins for the following Discworld names . . .

1 Untied Alchemists.

2 The Deosil Gate.

3 Walter Plinge.

4 Sto Lat.

5 We're Certainly Dwarfs (a Music With Rocks In band).

6 Ibid, the polymath philosopher.

7 The Wizards' Pleasaunce.

8 Saturday.

9 Koom Valley.

10 Amanita DeVice.

11 Chrononhotonthologos Street, Ankh-Morpork.

12 Mrs Rosie Palm, proprietor of a famous House of Negotiable Affection in the Shades.

ANSWERS

1 United Artists, celebrated movie studio. (*Moving Pictures*)

2 This gate is on the Turnwise as opposed to the Widdershins side of Ankh-Morpork. *Deasil* or *deosil* is an old Scots word meaning, well, the opposite direction to widdershins . . . literally, sunwise. (*The Colour of Magic*)

3 Walter Plinge is one of several traditional names put on theatre programmes when for some reason actors don't want to be billed under their real names. The Opera House does just this in *Maskerade*, and has an actual Walter Plinge as well.

4 Believe it or not, there is a Polish party song, roughly equivalent to 'For He's a Jolly Good Fellow', which begins: *Sto lat, sto lat, niech zyje, zyje nam.* ('Hundred years, hundred years, let him live for us' – i.e., wishing the jolly good fellow a long life.)

5 Refers to a not all that terrifically well known band called They Might Be Giants. (*Soul Music*)

6 *Ibid.*, short for *ibidem* ('in the same place'), features in the reference sections of learned works and papers on absolutely every subject, indicating a further reference to the last-named citation. Clearly this Ephebian philosopher knows something about everything. (*Pyramids*, *Small Gods*)

7 A nod to Parsons' Pleasure in Oxford, a fenced-off loop of the River Cherwell where university dons are traditionally allowed to bathe in the nude. Some still do (unlike the wizards), though intimidated by occasional parties of female students passing through in punts to see what they can see.

8 Baron Saturday, who dances in Genua on *Samedi Nuit Mort* (um, wasn't there once a TV show called *Saturday Night Live*?), is Baron Samedi, Lord of Graveyards, the *loa* or spirit whose province is death, sometimes represented by a top hat upon a cross . . . all elements in the heady voodoo stew concocted by Mrs Gogol. (*Witches Abroad*)

9 Cwm – pronounced Koom with 'oo' as in 'soot' – is Welsh for valley. Conceivably Koom Valley is a gesture to the multi-decker linguistic sandwich of Britain's Torpenhow Hill, literally Hillhillhill Hill.

10 'Device' (*Lords and Ladies*) is one of the surnames that can be found in those 17th-century lists of women charged with witchcraft – in particular, the celebrated 'Lancashire Witches'.* Garlick is another. So indeed is Nutter: see *Good Omens*, one of whose characters is also a Device . . . Anathema rather than Amanita. As for the Amanita, the name of a hallucinogenic mushroom seems a good bet for a witch.

11 From Henry Carey's play *Chrononhotonthologos: The Most Tragical Tragedy, That Ever was Tragediz'd by Any Company of Tragedians* (1734), a wild satire directed against too much empty rhetorical sound and fury on the stage. It includes this memorable enquiry about the hero: 'Aldiborontiphoscophornio! Where left you Chrononhotonthologos?'

12 To be going out with 'Mrs Palm and her five daughters' (also Mrs Palmer, Mrs Hand, etc.) is an oldish euphemism applied to those who are not Getting Any and, er, take the matter into their own hands.

---

* Lancashire. Lancre. Hmm. It is apparently pure coincidence that one notorious old-time witch-hunter, and persecutor of (in particular) Basque women, was Pierre de Lancre.

Faculty of
ESCHATOLOGY

A nice easy one: identify these final lines of Discworld texts:

1 There would always be another morning.

2 Death watched them walk away.

3 'It was *you* who foiled that hijacking over Chicago?'

4 And this, too, was happiness. Of a sort.

5 On the whole, he reflected, it could have been a lot worse.

6 Telling stories about heroes.

7 There didn't seem to be any alternative.

8 Now that would be a great adventure . . .

9 'That's not the way to do it.'

10 The ship fell onwards, into the scenery.

11 Of course, it is only a theory . . .

12 What more could anyone reasonably require?

Faculty of Eschatology
ANSWERS

1 *Sourcery.*

2 *Small Gods.*

3 *The Discworld Companion.*

4 *Eric.*

5 *Men at Arms.*

6 'Troll Bridge' (short story).

7 *The Colour of Magic.*

8 'Mapping the City' by Stephen Briggs, in *The Streets of Ankh-Morpork* (map booklet).

9 'Theatre of Cruelty' (short story; same final line in either version).

10 *Strata.* All right, it's not a novel about the *same* Discworld, but . . .

11 'Here Be Dragons . . . and Here . . . and Here . . .' in the booklet of *The Discworld Mapp.*

12 Terry Pratchett's introduction to this book.*

---

* A *really* cruel quizmaster could have put anything at all into question 12, with the answer: 'The question section of this quiz.' Be grateful for small mercies.

Faculty of LAIRAUDIENCE

Who or what, on these various occasions, is speaking?

1 SQUEAK.

2 SOMEONE IS PERFORMING THE RITE OF ASH . . .

3 I HAVE COME FOR THEE.

4 'Happiness.'

5 I HAVE COME TO GET YOU, YOU TERRIBLE ACTOR.

6 'Ftreat me rough . . . That'f the way I like it!'

7 GENTLEMEN . . . TAKE IT FROM THE TOP?

8

9 'Hat. Hat. Hat.'

10 TALKS LIKE THIS . . .

Faculty of Clairaudience
ANSWERS

1 The Death of Rats, *passim* (this is the easy one).

2 Mort at his most deathly, reaching the end of his apprenticeship. (*Mort*)

3 The demon Scrofula, standing in for Death in *The Colour of Magic*.

4 Death, not quite himself, being surprised by the sound of his own voice. (*Mort*)

5 Tomjon demonstrating how to talk in Death's hollow capitals. (*Wyrd Sisters*)

6 Cutwell's doorknocker, masochistically enjoying some hard knocks. (*Mort* again)

7 Susan (Death's, er, granddaughter) being Death's locum. (*Soul Music*)

8 Any inhabitant of Ankh-Morpork would instantly have recognized that sonorous knell of silence spoken by Old Tom, the cracked octiron bell of Unseen University.

9 The peculiar laugh of Mr Clete, the Musicians' Guild secretary. (*Soul Music*)

10 Albert describing Death. (*Mort*, yet again)

11 Oook.*

---

* Oh dear, we omitted the question – but it's clearly implicit in this outspokenly detailed answer. This is a Bonus Mark question.

Faculty of PHYSICK

Who or what might find themselves subject to the following afflictions?

1 The Plague of Frog.

2 Red Bugge.

3 Zigzag Throat.

4 The White Plague.

5 Wooden Udder.

6 Burning green fire in the belly, hot lead running in the bones, blistered skin and scorpions consuming the brain from within.

7 Root Fly.

8 Having Treacle Wormseed administered to them by Magrat Garlick.

9 The Black Tups.

10 Hydrophobia.

11 Licky End.

12 Being tragically crushed to death by a rogue elephant.

Faculty of Physick
ANSWERS

1 Persons in the Old Kingdom of Djelibeybi at some
stage during the last century. It should be noted that
the Plague of Frog was quite a big one, and got into
the air ducts and kept everyone awake for weeks.
(*Pyramids*)

2 Cows. (*Maskerade*)

3 Swamp dragons. (*Guards! Guards!*)

4 Anyone in Pseudopolis around the time of *The Colour
of Magic*'s final section. To the detriment of his
timetable, Death had to go and stalk the streets there.

5 Goats in the Ramtop Mountains. No extra marks for
deducing *nanny*-goats, but we appreciate the effort, we
really do. (*Equal Rites*)

6 In theory and as frantically commanded by a ship's
captain, a party of attacking Klatchian slave pirates. In
practice – owing to Rincewind's lack of magical ability
to fill the captain's order – no one. You can have a
mark for either answer. (*Sourcery*)

7 Cabbages. Never compliment a Sto Plains farmer on
how his cabbages look nice and ripe and yellow: this is
an indication of Root Fly. (*Soul Music*)

8 Sufferers from inflammation of the ears: Magrat is
under the impression that Treacle Wormseed is a
sovereign cure. (*Wyrd Sisters*)

9 Once again, swamp dragons – who are also prone to
Flameless Gripe, Slab Throat, Dry Lung, Storge,
Staggers, Heaves, Weeps, Stones, Blowing Up Rather
Messily, and many more. (*Guards! Guards!*)

10 Wizards of Krull, trained from birth on dehydrated water until their loathing for liquid becomes a physical force: they can make rainclouds go away or, by sheer strength of revulsion, levitate themselves, though only over water. But they die young through inability to live with themselves. (*The Colour of Magic*)

11 Licky End affects only pregnant sheep. It is thus a further example of Life's and Nature's unfairness that Gaspode the Wonder Dog should suffer from it. (*Men at Arms*)

12 Anyone questioning the legitimacy of the Duke of Sto Helit's plans for usurping the Sto Lat throne was liable to find that being tragically crushed to death by rogue elephants could be catching.* (*Mort*)

---

* Just as, in *Wyrd Sisters*, falling down a flight of steps with a dagger in the back also proves contagious. It is a disease caused by unwise opening of the mouth.

Faculty of
LEY LINES

What or who is a possible Discworld connection of . . .

1 Galileo?

2 Mr Justice Cocklecarrot and the Twelve Red-Bearded Dwarfs?

3 Andrew Lang?

4 Gollum?

5 Science-fiction authors Thomas M. Disch and John T. Sladek?

6 St Simon Stylites?

7 Hans Christian Andersen's most sensitive Princess?

8 The novel *Erewhon* by Samuel Butler?

9 Albertus Magnus?

10 Herman Bondi, Thomas Gold and Fred Hoyle?

ANSWERS

1   'Nevertheless it does move,' Galileo supposedly said
    after being forced by the Inquisition to recant his belief
    that the Earth orbited the Sun . . . but he cautiously
    said it under his breath *and* in Italian (*Eppur si muove*).
    Elsewhere, the Quisition of the Church of the Great
    God Om takes a hard line with those asserting the
    heresy that Discworld is flat and propped up by four
    elephants standing on a space-traversing turtle (which
    it is). And freethinkers like the philosopher Didactylos
    say, 'The Turtle moves.' (*Small Gods*)

2   Rincewind the wizard. The first bearer of this name in
    modern literature was Churm Rincewind, one of the 12
    red-bearded dwarfs who plagued Mr Justice
    Cocklecarrot in the 1930s (and later) *By the Way*
    newspaper columns by Beachcomber (J.B. Morton). It
    could have been worse: the others claimed to be called
    Sophus Barkayo-Tong, Amaninter Axling, Farjole
    Merrybody, Guttergorm Guttergormpton, Badly
    Oronparser, Cleveland Zackhouse, Molonay
    Tubilderborst, Edeledel Edel, Scorpion de Rooftrouser,
    Listenis Youghapt and Frums Gillygottle. By the way, in
    The Colour of Magic Rincewind plans at one point to
    'take the coast road to Chirm'.

3   Andrew Lang edited a series of fairy-story collections
    beginning with *The Blue Fairy Book* (1889) and
    continuing through various colours. In Discworld,
    naturally, there is *The Octarine Fairy Book*. (*The
    Colour of Magic*)

4   Many readers' eyes narrowed in suspicion at the small,
    nameless, grey, clammy creature in the underground
    river of *Witches Abroad*, who paddles up to the
    witches' boat and announces "Ullo . . . It'sss my
    birthday.' He doesn't get any further, which is just as
    well.

5   Disch and Sladek collaborated on a 1968 satirical
     thriller called *Black Alice*; the legendarily powerful and
     thankfully dead Discworld witch Aliss Demurrage is
     universally known as Black Aliss.*

6   St Ungulant in *Small Gods* is the Discworld analogue
     of Stylites (*d.* AD 460), or of any other saint who simil-
     arly abjured the world by spending his life sitting on a
     pole or pillar – not, when you think about it, an activity
     that greatly enhances the world's spiritual well-being.

7   The heroine of Andersen's 'The Princess on the Pea'
     demonstrates her royal sensitivity by being unable to
     sleep owing to the lumpiness of one pea beneath her
     stack of 20 mattresses and 20 feather beds. The
     Discworld version, picked up via the usual morphic
     Chinese Whispers, has 'princesses so noble they, they
     could pee through a dozen mattresses' (Albert in *Mort*).
     There's a slightly less tortured allusion to the story in
     Guards! Guards! Bonus mark if you cited both.

8   Butler's imaginary land Erewhon is an anagram
     approximating to a backwards spelling of 'Nowhere';
     The Colour of Magic fleetingly refers to 'Ecalpon', a
     reversal of 'Noplace'.

9   Perhaps echoed by that equally celebrated figure of
     antiquated learning, Alberto Malich – founder of
     Unseen University and latterly a skivvy in the house of
     Death. (*Mort, Soul Music*)

10   Bondi, Gold and Hoyle proposed the Steady State (as
     opposed to Big Bang) theory of our universe. The non-
     Big Bang school of Discworld cosmology opines that
     the great turtle supporting the world moves through
     space at 'a uniform crawl, or steady gait'. (*The Colour
     of Magic*)

---

* A genuine coincidence, says a bemused Terry Pratchett ... who had
merely noted the frequency of the name Alice in lists of arraigned 17th-
century witches, and then added the 'Black'.

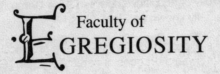 Faculty of
EGREGIOSITY

Who or what is the odd one out in each set?

1 Cobb, Pewmet, Wimple, Cock, Snood.

2 Galder Weatherwax, Cutangle, Coin, Mustrum Ridcully.

3 Galder Weatherwax, Tethis, Corporal Disuse, Weems.

4 Ipslore the Red, Exquisitor Vorbis, Deccan Ribobe, Drum Billet.

5 Glod, Carrot, Swires, Constable Cuddy.

6 Glod, Gimli in *The Lord of the Rings*, Alberich in *The Ring of the Nibelungen*, Rumpelstiltskin in *Grimms' Fairy Tales*.

7 Glod, Glod, Glod, Glod, Glod, Glod.

8 A Big Troll and Some Other Trolls, The Band With Rocks In, We're a Rubbish Band, Dwarfs With Altitude, Ande Supporting Bands, The Blots.

9 Suck, Surreptitious Fabric, Ande Supporting Bands, The Whom, Dwarfs With Altitude, Lead Balloon.

10 The Blots, Suck, Surreptitious Fabric, Ande Supporting Bands, The Whom, Lead Balloon.

Faculty of Egregiosity
ANSWERS

1   With the exception of Wimple, all are technical terms for male swamp dragons of particular ages. (*Guards! Guards!*)

2   All Archchancellors of Unseen University, you said in puzzlement? Check *The Light Fantastic*: in that work, Weatherwax is mysteriously listed only as Chancellor and *not* Archchancellor.* (*Voice of the Reader*: 'Anorak-wearing pedant!')

3   All vanished suspiciously in the vicinity of the ever-ferocious sentient Luggage. Only Tethis in *The Colour of Magic* ever got out again.

4   All die near the beginnings of Discworld books – except Vorbis, who dies to general applause near the end of *Small Gods*.

5   All are dwarfs (Carrot admittedly being an unusually tall *honorary* dwarf) except Swires (*The Light Fantastic*), who is a gnome and a lower** form of life altogether.

6   All are dwarfs except Gimli, because Tolkien preferred to spell it 'dwarves' – a neologism carefully avoided in Discworld.

7   Half a mark for any answer along the lines of 'none of them, it's a traditional dwarf drinking song engraved by a shaky speller'. One mark for inferring that one of the Glods is the dwarf horn-player Glod Glodsson in *Soul Music* – while the others result from the misprinted spell that transmuted things into Glod, an entirely

---

* However, in a piece of retrospective fixing, the passage in *Lords and Ladies* which establishes Galder as Granny's distant cousin (whom she never actually met) promotes him to Archchancellor.

** Height about six inches.

different dwarf who was soured by being relentlessly and repeatedly duplicated. (*Witches Abroad*)

8 In *Soul Music*, only We're a Rubbish Band is not actually at any time the adopted name of a Music With Rocks In group.

9 All different names of the same terrible group, except for Dwarfs With Altitude.

10 All the same group, but Ande Supporting Bands is the only one of these names under which they actually play on stage.

Faculty of
NUMEROLOGY

It is completely unknown that Discworld has its own version of the celebrated counting song 'Green Grow the Rushes-o'. Naturally, the most extended verse begins 'I'll sing you twelve-o, Brown flows the Ankh-o . . . What are your twelve-o? Twelve for the something-or-other' – and goes rapidly downhill to 'One is one is Great A'Tuin and evermore shall be so'. From the list below you should be able to reconstruct the lines (which don't all scan very well, or at all*) and put them in order.

?	Stone dancers.
?	Yoked oxen.
?	Shadows on the wall.
?	Spelter's level.
?	Moving pictures.
?	Books of the Prophets.
?	Strokes of nine-ish.
?	cc of mouse blood.
?	Month of Ember.
?	Rincewind's number.
?	Fast-painting demons.
?	Crippled onion.

---

* Singers are expected to gloss over this by inordinate loudness and a lot of quaffing.

Faculty of Numerology
ANSWERS

Twelve for the strokes of nine-ish – at the Genua ball, midnight struck at about nine when Nanny Ogg and Casanunda fiddled with the clock mechanism. (*Witches Abroad*)

Eleven for the month of Ember – the 11th month of the Discworld's 13. (*The Discworld Companion*)

Ten for the moving pictures – Moving Pictures was the tenth Discworld-series book to be published.

Nine for the crippled Onion – a nine-card run 'cripples' a Great Onion in the game of Cripple Mr Onion. (*Witches Abroad*)

Eight for the eight Dancers – the Lancre circle stones in *Lords and Ladies*.

Seven-A for Rincewind's number – his room number at Unseen University, since *seven plus one* or *twice four* is unlucky for wizards.

Seven for the Seven Books of the Prophets – the Septateuch. (*Small Gods*)

Six for the shadows on the wall – of the dragon-vaporized Shades muggers. (*Guards! Guards!*)

Five for the wizard Spelter's level – of wizardry. (*Sourcery*)

Four cc of mouse blood – for the Rite of AshkEnte, streamlined version.

Three the yokèd oxen – Three Yokèd Oxen is a character in *Interesting Times*.

Two fast-painting demons, in a picture box-o – in *Moving Pictures* two demons paint the movie frames while four more blow hard to dry them.

One is one is Great A'Tuin and evermore shall be so – but you don't get a mark for that one, cully.

Faculty of
ELDRITCH SYNCHRONICITY

Who or what from our world is the original of . . .

1   The ichor god Bel-Shamharoth, in *The Colour of Magic*?

2   Mr so-called Amazing Maurice and His Educated Rodents, in *Reaper Man*?

3   Lord Vetinari of Ankh-Morpork?

4   The Duchess of Lancre, in *Wyrd Sisters*?

5   Imp y Celyn, of the Band With Rocks In?

6   *Blown Away*, in *Moving Pictures*?

7   The Chant of the Trodden Spiral (as applied to 66-megalith stone circles), in *The Light Fantastic*?

8   That fearful grimoire the *Liber Paginarum Fulvarum*?

9   Creosote, Seriph of Al Khali, in *Sourcery*?

10 The Guardian of the Portal of the Silver Screen, in *Moving Pictures*?

Faculty of Eldritch Synchronicity
ANSWERS

In a way these are all trick questions using the same trick. Terry Pratchett would very reasonably be annoyed if you insisted he simply pinched his material from X or Y or Z. Indeed, the Discworld Theory of Stories suggests that when someone here and someone *there* seem strangely alike, this is probably not because either is imitating the other but because they're both instances of the identical morphic character wossname which first emerged in something primordial and single-celled.

So, if you said 'None' right down the page you should get full marks. But examiners don't like smartarses, and what they quite wrongly wanted you to say was:

1   H.P. Lovecraft's Cthulhu, or any of his loathsome, blasphemous relatives like Azathoth or Yog-Sothoth. If you answered *Ph'nglui mglw'nafh Cthulhu R'lyeh wgah'nagl fhtagn*, lose half a mark for showing off.

2   The Pied Piper.

3   Half a mark each for mentioning (a) any of the de Medicis; (b) Machiavelli. If you didn't get (a) that means you didn't read Terry's Introduction to this book – *shame* on you!

4   Lady Macbeth.*

5   Damn it, it was on my tip of my tongue, there *must* be some rock star whose name sounds a bit like Bud of the Holly . . .

6   *Gone with the Wind.*

7   A computer program.

* Whose first name, redolent of bonny Scottishness and seductive wiles, was Gruoch.

8 Another tricky one. Earthly students of ritual magic seem curiously ill-informed on (to translate literally) *The Book of Yellow Pages*.

9 Omar Khayyám of *Rubáiyát* fame, but without the talent. Bonus mark for also mentioning the legendarily wealthy Croesus: 'as rich as Croesus' naturally becomes 'as rich as Creosote' on Discworld. (Considering what creosote actually is, there is an underlying flavour of Oil Sheikh here.)

10 Someone thought this prize statuette looked remarkably like their Uncle Oscar – or was it Oswald . . . Osric . . . Osbert?

Faculty of PARAZOOLOGY

Concerning the strange creepy creatures of
Discworld and its environs . . .

1 Gets through its food so fast that it comes whizzing out
   the other side and ricochets off the wall.

2 Exists in only two dimensions and eats mathematicians.

3 A witch's familiar that was interestingly named
   Lightfoot.

4 A shy, grey-brown bird of the coot family.

5 Quadruped whose actions soldiers are traditionally
   advised to imitate when going into battle.

6 Fatally fond of oatmeal mingled with essence of spikkle.

7 They graze on the contents of choice books and leave,
   behind them, piles of small slim volumes of literary
   criticism.

8 Officially a dark and dangerous spirit, this was black and
   quite the biggest one Nanny Ogg had ever seen – 'and
   I've seen a few in my time'.

9 Three years after his nasty encounter with a werewolf, the
   mugger Bundo Prung was killed in a far-off country when
   one of these fell on his head.

10 Kept biting the top of the deodorant bottle.

ANSWERS

1 The .303 bookworm. (*Pyramids*)

2 The Shadowing Lemma. (*Men at Arms*)

3 A tortoise, or tortoyse – incredibly old and knowing many secrets, or so the salesman told its purchaser Magrat. (*Wyrd Sisters*)

4 The gaskin . . . according, at least, to the *Dictionary of Eye-Watering Words*. (*Guards! Guards!*)

5 The Lancre Reciprocating Fox. (*Lords and Ladies*)

6 Rats – Miss Flitworth's infallible remedy. (*Reaper Man*)

7 Critters – relatively harmless denizens of L-space. (*Guards! Guards!*)

8 Legba, Mrs Gogol's black cockerel – the only animal ever recorded to have successfully stared down the appalling cat Greebo. (*Witches Abroad*)

9 An armadillo. (*Men at Arms*)

10 Medusa's underarm snakes . . . a little-considered aspect of having these creatures instead of hair.* (*Soul Music*)

---

* Don't extrapolate *any* further, now.

Faculty of 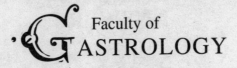GASTROLOGY

Another simple theme quiz for you to chew on. Just identify the, er, things that the questions identify . . .

1 Strangely appropriate as an accompaniment to click watching. (You need a No. 3 crucible and some oil.)

2 Hurled at ballistic speed, this smelly object stunned a bat that was more than it seemed.

3 Purveyed by Ardrothy Longstaff of Sator Square, they were allegedly full of personality.

4 The only recipe in Nanny Ogg's book that does not in some way relate to . . . goings-on. ('No, I tell a lie . . .')

5 The difficulty is to stop spelling it.

6 Intensely durable products manufactured under the Captain Eightpanther brand name.

7 The named version costs 50 per cent more than the regular one.

8 Tantalizingly smelled on a flying rock 500 feet above-ground.

9 What a marooned wizard hoped for when promised all the earthly and sensual pleasures of his dreams.

10 Allegedly it both helps you see in the dark and ensures you've got something to look at.

Faculty of Gastrology
ANSWERS

Obviously this was the foodie quiz paper . . .

1 Banged grains. (*Moving Pictures*)

2 A garlic sausage, traditionally effective against vampires. (*Witches Abroad*)

3 Pork pies. (*Sourcery*)

4 Porridge. But even that has Nanny Ogg's special honey mixture in it. (*Maskerade*)

5 Banananana, or banananana, etc., etc. . . . *passim.*

6 Captain Eightpanther's Traveller's Digestives – biscuits with the texture of diamondwood. (*The Colour of Magic*)

7 At the Curry Gardens in Ankh-Morpork: 'Curry with Meat 10p. Curry with Named Meat 15p.' (*Soul Music*)

8 Fried bacon. (*The Light Fantastic*)

9 Potatoes, mashed. Yes, of course it was Rincewind. (*Interesting Times*)

10 Nanny Ogg's Carrot and Oyster Pie. (*Lords and Ladies*)

Faculty of EUREKA!

Which Discworld novels first described the
following interesting inventions (or their close
equivalents)?

1   The electronic flashgun.

2   The Post-it™ note.

3   The better mousetrap.

4   A working microscope.

5   Hypersonic jet flight.

6   The tank.

7   The hydraulic ram.

8   The video security camera.

9   Subliminal advertising.

10 Penicillin.

ANSWERS

1 *The Colour of Magic*, using over-stimulated salamanders.

2 *Men at Arms*. The great inventor Leonard of Quirm synthesized a suitable glue from boiled slugs.

3 *Moving Pictures*. Details of the better mousetrap are unknown owing to the fact that 1000 elephants immediately beat a path to, and through, the inventor's door. This scientific principle was first laid down by Ralph Waldo Emerson in the 19th century: 'If a man write a better book, preach a better sermon, or make a better mousetrap than his neighbour, though he build his house in the woods, the world will make a beaten path to his door.'

4 *Soul Music*. The device with which Stibbons demonstrates to Archchancellor Ridcully how incredibly many tiny animals live in a single drop of the river Ankh. Ridcully reasons that anything supporting that much life *has* to be healthy.

5 *Guards! Guards!* Errol the swamp dragon reconfigures and reverses his flame-producing digestive system to produce a powerful, hot thrust from an unconventional outlet. (Death's horse goes much faster when required, of course, but does not as far as is known use jets.)

6 Half a mark for citing *Small Gods* and Urn's steam-driven Moving Turtle; a full mark for Lavaeolus's imaginative extrapolation from the treadmill of Hell in *Eric*.

7 *Pyramids* – as an analogy to help explain how a pyramid pumps time against the natural current.

8 *The Light Fantastic.* Perhaps a bit beyond Discworld technology, this is seen only in a Magic Shop capable of inter-universal travel.

9 *Moving Pictures.* Dibbler extrapolated from the effectiveness of a subliminal flash to the surely much greater impact of showing a plate of spare ribs (in Harga's Special Peanut Sauce) for five whole subliminal minutes . . .

10 *Lords and Ladies.* Magrat worries about a wound being infected and asks if the cook has any mouldy bread. This is a genuine bit of folk medicine anticipating fact: centuries before Sir Alexander Fleming, European housewives reputedly kept a mouldy loaf on hand and used wet slices to poultice wounds. With luck, the home-made culture would include penicillin. Without luck . . . many moulds also produce carcinogens. (See, for example, *The Wordsworth Dictionary of Medical Folklore*, edited by Carol Ann Rinzler.)

Faculty of
LINGUISTICS

How would you translate the following esoteric
(pardon my Klatchian) terms from the languages
indicated?

1   Agatean pictogram: *[urinating dog]*.

2   Ankh-Morporkian: *welchet*.

3   Troll: *oograah*.

4   Generic Foreign: *olé!*

5   Archaic Ankh-Morporkian: FABRICATE DIEM, PVNC.

6   Another Sort of Foreign: *Der Flabberghast*.

7   Circle Sea dialect: Skund (as in Forest of).

8   Monkey: 'Oook!'

9   Old Omnian: *Cuius testiculos habes, habeas cardia et cerebellum.*

10 Dwarf: *[foul insult censored from this book at the request of the Campaign for Equal Heights].**

---

* Oh all right: *b'zugda-hiara*.

Faculty of Linguistics
ANSWERS

1 An exclamation mark, possibly doubled and underlined. (*Interesting Times*)

2 'A type of waistcoat worn by certain clock-makers', according to the *Dictionary of Eye-Watering Words*. Among the frightful penalties in the rituals of the Elucidated Brethren of the Ebon Night is to have one's welchet torn asunder with many hooks and one's figgin* placed upon a spike. (*Guards! Guards!*)

3 Vegetation – *any* vegetation. Hence the confusion when Ruby hints to her aspiring troll lover Detritus that he should woo her with nice *oograah* (flowers) and he duly offers a gigantic uprooted *oograah* (tree). (*Moving Pictures*) On the other hand, trolls have 5400 distinct words for varieties of rock.

4 'With milk.' (*Reaper Man, Witches Abroad*)

5 Motto of the Night Watch: 'To Protect and To Serve' (Sergeant Colon's translation in *Guards! Guards!*).

6 'The bat.' Also translated, to Terry Pratchett's surprise, as 'word found in a Dudley Moore song from *Beyond the Fringe*, 1961' – only there it was *Die Flabberghast*. Not a lot of people want to know that. (*Witches Abroad*)

7 'Your Finger You Fool.' (*The Light Fantastic*)

8 'The examiner is about to have his head violently pounded against adjacent ceilings, walls and floors by an annoyed *ape*, for using the m-word.'

9 Official translation: 'When you have their full attention in your grip, their hearts and minds will follow.' (*Small Gods*)

10 'Lawn ornament.'

* See footnote in that copy of *Guards! Guards!* you illicitly smuggled into the examination room.

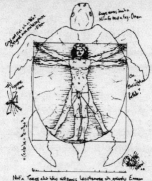

Faculty of
ACRONYMICS

Expand upon . . .

1   Y M R-C-I-G-B-S A.

2   MSDOS.

3   X.

4   N (as in 'I don't do the N word').

5   AFP.

6   DMHD.

7   YMPA.

8   TWA.

9   XXXX.

10   α - Ω.

11   &U.

12   CMOT.

ANSWERS

1 Young Men's Reformed-Cultists-of-the-Ichor-God-Bel-Shamharoth Association. (*Pyramids, Soul Music*)

2 *Mallificarum Sumpta Diabolicite Occularis Singularum* – the Book of Ultimate Control, in *Eric*. What else could it possibly stand for?

3 As a middle initial, stands for 'someone who has a cool and exciting middle initial'. (*Maskerade*)

4 Presumably – since the speaker is a raven whose nominal owner calls him Quoth – 'Nevermore'.* (*Soul Music*)

5 Oh dear, it had to get a mention somewhere: alt.fan.pratchett, the Usenet newsgroup where they talk about this kind of thing.

6 Disembowel-Myself-Honourably Dibhala, one of Cut-My-Own-Throat's morphic clones. (*Interesting Times*)

7 Young Men's Pagan Association – mentioned, though not as an acronym, in *The Light Fantastic*.

8 Three Witches Airborne, in *Witches Abroad*. No marks for citing the label with the 'powerful travelling rune TWA' picked up by the Luggage when visiting our Earthly plane in *The Colour of Magic*, since we are not told what this stands for. Ahem.

---

* Those given to brooding gloomily on the state of modern education will be unsurprised that, although Poe's best-known poem *The Raven* inspired a full-length Roger Corman movie whose tagline is indeed 'Quoth the Raven, "Nevermore"', rather few readers seem to realize what the N-word actually is . . .

9   *Terra Australis Incognita*, or any plausible paraphrase.*

10 Alpha to Omega, like A to Z: the trade name of one
    locally produced Streete Mappe of Ankh-Morpork.
    (*Interesting Times*)

11 'And You' . . . Discworld band name echoing our
    world's 'You Too' or U2. (*Soul Music*)

12 It'd be Cutting My Own Throat to spell out the answer
    to that one . . . No marks for saying 'Cripple Mr Onion
    Tournament', which would have been a *trick question*
    and *unethical*.

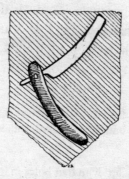

---

*   Although there's something curiously Australian about XXXX, the
flat Discworld naturally has no austral or southern direction. XXXX is
also known (e.g., in *Interesting Times* and on the official Mapp) as
Terror Incognita.

Faculty of HYSTERON PROTERON

A legendary and perhaps mythical Oxford philosophy paper once asked: 'Is this a question?' The response 'No, but this is an answer' is supposed to have won a top First . . . Right: the following are not questions. Now go ahead and tackle them.

1 It holds them down and shows them pictures of its children until their brains implode.

2 IN PAIRS.

3 A small card with four holes in it.

4 *Rincewind:* Ah . . . I think I know that one.

5 This is one of them personality questions, ain't it?

6 No one's ever said . . . I suppose so.

7 That's better. That's more according to the script.

8 Ponder Stibbons.

9 Nothing so pleasant, but –

10 Somewhere in Howondaland, isn't it?

11 What duck?

12 Mrs Cake.

QUESTIONS

The sensitive, intelligent reader will have seen at once that, placing the cart subtly before the horse, this quiz consists of the answers or replies to various queries in Discworld books. Clearly you need to provide some approximation to the questions, as follows . . .

1   How does the monster Tshup Aklathep, Infernal Star Toad with A Million Young, torture its victims to death? (*Moving Pictures*)

2   'How do you get all those coins?' – Mort to Death. (*Mort*)

3   2 x 2? – as programmed into Unseen's computer Hex. (*Soul Music*)

4 '*What the hell is that thing with all the legs?*'– Ridcully to Rincewind. (*Interesting Times*)

5 'Gytha Ogg, your house is on fire, what's the first thing you'd try to take out?' – Granny Weatherwax. (*Maskerade*)

6 'Are you magical?' – Rincewind to a tree. (*The Light Fantastic*)

7 'Why have you summoned me, then?' – Susan to Ridcully. (*Soul Music*)

8 'What is your name?' – Unseen University examination paper. (*Moving Pictures*)

9 'We'll all be eaten by things with tentacles for faces, right?' – Bethan to Wert and/or Rincewind. (*The Light Fantastic*)

10 'Have you ever heard of Ethics?' – Brutha to Om. (*Small Gods*)

11 WHY ARE YOU WALKING AROUND WITH THAT DUCK? – Guess Who to the Duck Man. (*Soul Music*)

12 Which Discworld boarding-house keeper cursed with erratic precognition would have no trouble at all with this section?

SPOONFETCHERS
LEECHES
THE LITTLE SUCKERS

Faculty of
'CONTINUUM
ONTOLOGY

Continue or complete these simple sequences by
filling in the blank item . . .

1 2, 2, 58%, 94%, ——.

2 Trouser of Sanctity, Red Cords of Intellect, Wheels of
Torment, ——, Thuribles of Destiny.

3 *TCOM*, *TLF*, *M*, *S*, ——, *IT*.

4 Anger, Jealousy, Bestiality, ——, Deviousness.

5 91, 73, 68, 37, ——.

6 Aqueduct, Fishing line, Weir, Dam, ——.

7 1433, 1456, 1463, ——, 1470, 1690.

8 Slumpie, Jammie Devils, ——, Distressed Pudding,
Clooty Dumplings, Knuckle Sandwich.

9 8, 8, 8, 8th, 8th, ——, 8th.

10 Skillet, ——, ——, ——, ——, Patel.

ANSWERS

1 00.00 – from Magrat's personal stocktaking of arms, legs, existential dread, randomized guilt and witchcraft level. (*Lords and Ladies*)

2 Axles of the Universal Lemon – from the sequence of ritual objects employed by the Elucidated Brethren. (*Guards! Guards!*)

3 *E* – title initials of novels featuring Rincewind.

4 Covetousness – these being the forenames of various Carter sons in *Lords and Ladies* and *Maskerade* (their parents having got the wrong idea about boys' names after calling their daughters Hope, Chastity, etc.).

5 19 – Albert's countdown record of his remaining lifetimer days. (*Soul Music*)

6 Bridge – Rincewind's attempts to name a card game that in his language is 'thing you put across a river' never actually get to this word. But it is, ahem, Implied. (*The Light Fantastic*)

7 1465 – these are the dates of Licensed Premises (Hygiene) Acts formerly applying in Ankh-Morpork. (*Guards! Guards!*)

8 Fikkun haddock – from a list of local delicacies in Wellcome to Ankh-Morpork, Citie of One Thousand Surprises. (*Men at Arms*)

9 7 – see the opening paragraphs of *Sourcery*.

10 Wang, Yrxle!yt, Bunglestiff, Cwmlad – proprietors listed on the sign of the magic shop in *The Light Fantastic*. Under the circumstances, you can have a mark for managing any two or more of these.

Faculty of
CLAIRAUDIENCE II

Again, who or what, on these various occasions, is
speaking? Be careful.

1 YES.

2 *So. At the last, you fail me.*

3 I AM ALWAYS AROUND.

4 *It's not that, then?*

5 I DON'T CARE WHAT IT SAYS . . . I NEVER LAID A FINGER ON
HIM.

6 *Put me down on the floor and stand back.*

7 WELL, THEY DO SAY DEATH CHANGES THINGS . . . HAD TO
WORK MY FINGERS TO THE BONE. (You've guessed who, but
which book?)

8 *I. Shall I Smite Them?*

9 GIVE IT TO US.

10 *You're mine. We don't need him any more.*

Faculty of Clairaudience II
ANSWERS

1 Azrael. The large rather than small capitals were a Clue. (*Reaper Man*)

2 The late wizard Ipslore the Red and/or his staff, towards the end of *Sourcery*.

3 Death, but no marks unless correctly identified as not the Death of Discworld but that of our own Earth, in the short story 'Turntables of the Night'.

4 Pestilence in *Sourcery*, mysteriously lapsing from his characteristic italics – in both British editions, the Gollancz hardback and the Corgi paperback, at any rate. Sorry. We are growing obsessive.

5 Death, but no marks unless correctly identified as the Death of (another version of) our own Earth, in *Good Omens*. The 'him' is Elvis Presley.

6 The Lady (Luck), manifesting through a frog. (*The Colour of Magic*)

7 Death in . . . no, not *Mort* but the heavily rewritten Discworld Big Comic adaptation of *Mort*.

8 Om. (*Small Gods*)

9 The Things in the Dungeon Dimensions, speaking to Esk. (*Equal Rites*)

10 The perhaps imagined, soundless voice of the Gonne. (*Men at Arms*)

Faculty of MODERN HISTORY

1 What dread image was captured by the magic picture-taking box when it was used in the unspeakable temple of the ichor god Bel-Shamharoth?

2 Where would you find a staircase whose risers average only 1.08 inches in height?

3 Who was the greatest mathematician in the world?

4 Where would you look for Room 3B?

5 How long did the Octavo stay inside the Luggage?

6 Who was the greatest storyteller in the history of Discworld?

7 Why was it called Hide Park?

8 What was prosecuted for obscuring the light during Frenzied Earl Hargarth's investiture ceremony?

9 Which phenomenon of Nature practised for hours in front of a glacier?

10 How many Wonders of the World are there on Discworld?

11 How large is the standing army of the Kingdom of Lancre?

12 What, according to wizards, is the lowliest grade of *real* magic-user?

Faculty of Modern History
ANSWERS

1   Rincewind's thumb. (*The Colour of Magic*)

2   Lose a mark for any guess involving Bloody Stupid Johnson. The Tower of Art at Unseen University is 800 feet tall and has 8,888 steps, and so . . .

3   The camel You Bastard, in *Pyramids*.

4   Unseen University is the correct place to look, although you wouldn't find Room 3B. It is the unlocatable venue for all the university's virtual lectures – i.e., those unattended by students, or lecturers. (*Interesting Times*)

5   'It ate a book of spells last year. Sulked for three days and then spat it out,' says Rincewind in *Sourcery*. We assume it's the same spellbook . . .

6   Copolymer of Ephebe. Who can forget his immortal account of the Trojan War, Discworld version? 'It was wossname's idea, the one with the limp. Yes. The limp in his leg, I mean. Did I mention him? There'd been this

fight. No, that was the other one, I think. Yes. Anyway, this wooden pig, damn clever idea, they made it out of thing. Tip of my tongue. Wood . . .' (*Pyramids*)

7   Because it covered one hide of land, being the amount ploughable by one man with three oxen on a wet Thursday. (*Soul Music*)

8   A small cloud that covered the sun. It was sentenced to be stoned to death, and 31 people were killed in the effort. (*Guards! Guards!*)

9   The theatrically ambitious storm in *Wyrd Sisters*.

10 'More Than Seven.' (*Pyramids*)

11 Lancre has a standing army of one – Shawn Ogg – modulating to zero when he's lying down. (*Lords and Ladies*)

12 Thaumaturgists, unschooled lowlifes who can barely be trusted to wash out an alembic; they get the dirty, hazardous jobs like going and fetching mandrake roots. Witches, according to wizards, don't count. (*Equal Rites*)

Faculty of
EGREGIOSITY II

Again, who or what is the odd one out in each set?

1   Ghoul, werewolf, dwarf, banshee, troll.

2   Ghoul, banshee, vampire, troll, zombie.

3   The Mended Drum, The Goat & Bush, The Bucket, The Silver Eel, The Crimson Leech.

4   The Broken Drum, The Jolly Cabbage, The Quene's Hed, The Mended Drum, The Duke's Head.

5   Chert, Tethis, Kwartz, Bauxite, Jasper, Scree.

6   Foul Ole Ron, Offler the Crocodile God, Mr Ixolite, Cutwell's doorknocker, Cornice-overlooking-Broadway.

7   Death, The Eight of Octograms, The Importance of Washing the Hands, The Dome of the Sky, The Wheel of Fortune.

8   Octiron, Kring, stones with holes in them, Rincewind, the Ramtops.

9   Figgin, Gaskin, Moules, Welchet.

10 Welchet, Moules, Gaskin, Figgin.

Dead? Depressed?
Feel like starting it all again?
Then why not come along to the
FRESH START CLUB
Thursdays, 12 pm, 668 Elm Street
EVERY BODY WELCOME

Faculty of Egregiosity II
ANSWERS

1 Only banshees are not proposed and/or recruited as useful additions to the Ankh-Morpork Night Watch (and also a convenient sop to minority rights groups) in *Men at Arms*.

2 All represented in Reg Shoe's Fresh Start Club ('Dead? Depressed? Feel like starting it all again?') in *Reaper Man* . . . except trolls.

3 All are Discworld pubs except The Silver Eel, which is in another famous fantasy universe altogether (Fritz Leiber's Nehwon).

4 Again, all are Discworld pubs, but only The Jolly Cabbage has just the one name (the two Drums being the same pub, and likewise the two Heads).

5 All are trolls: Tethis from *The Colour of Magic* is unusual in not having a 'rock' or 'stone' name, but then he *is* a sea troll. In Greek mythology, Tethys was the Titan associated with the sea, who married her brother Oceanus and had 3000 sons (the world's rivers) plus 3000 daughters (one water nymph per river). Presumably the titanic couple got on fairly well together.

6 Foul Ole Ron is the one without a speech impediment. Brain impediment is another matter.

7 These are all Caroc cards except The Wheel of Fortune, which (like Death) is also in our own Tarot pack but (unlike Death) hasn't yet turned up as a Discworld card.

8 All magical, or supposedly so, with the glaringly incompetent exception of Rincewind.*

9 Yes, they all feature in the same sentence in *Guards! Guards!* and they're all allegedly in the *Dictionary of Eye-Watering Words*, but Gaskin is also the name of a Discworld character. However, see the next answer.

10 Yes, these *are* the same words as in the last question, and you can regard answers 9 and 10 as interchangeable. The alternative odd one out is Welchet, since Figgin(s), Gaskin and Moules can all be found in the complete *Oxford English Dictionary* – though with slightly different definitions from those in *Eye-Watering Words*.

---

* This is official and axiomatic. Certain episodes in *The Light Fantastic* and *Sourcery* may encourage rebellious quibbling, but these can be explained away, respectively, by the Spell and by the world-pervading presence of Sourcery.

Faculty of
PARAPSYCHOLOGY

Attune your mind to the infinite, flex your astral
muscles, and consider these awesome enigmas
from beyond time and space . . .

1 Who would wear false false beards?

2 If the Discworld had a feature called the Great Gre, what
   would it be like?

3 How would you treat a disembodied spirit to a stiff drink?

4 Why were the Gods engaged in an aeons-old battle with
   the Ice Giants?

5 What is the relationship of shopping malls to cities?

6 How many different octograms are there in the
   Discworld's mystic Ching Aling?

7 What is a sure-fire wizardly way to recognize mushrooms
   that are not good to eat?

8 What dissolves spircles?

9 What is impossible to count even though there is only one
   of it?

10 Where did a noble comet die as a prince flamed across
   the sky?

ANSWERS

1   Members of the wizardly faculty of Unseen University
    when they sneak out to the clicks in disguise –
    disguise, that is, of their real beards. What you do, as
    the Lecturer in Recent Runes explains, is to take two
    pieces of wire, twiddle them into your sideburns, then
    loop them over your ears rather clumsily . . . and you
    look just like someone wearing a very badly made false
    beard. (*Moving Pictures*)

2   Probably a swamp. The Earth desert called the Great
    Erg has its Discworld counterpart in the Great Nef,
    which is 'fen' backwards, so the Great Gre would
    logically be . . .

3   Mrs Cake's method is to kill a glass of whisky by
    setting fire to it, thus allowing her ectoplasmic friend to
    enjoy the – er – spirit of the spirit. (*Reaper Man*)

4   The Ice Giants had refused to return the lawnmower.
    The litigation is another issue, arising from the fact that
    the Ice Giants also refused to turn their radio down.
    (*The Light Fantastic*)

5   Predator and prey – as demonstrated in *Reaper Man*
    and all over an obscure non-Discworld province called
    Britain.

6   Good question! One mark if you reasoned that, on
    Earth, the *I Ching*'s set of hexagrams covers all
    possible permutations of 6 lines which may each be
    either broken or unbroken, giving 2^6 or 64 patterns –
    and that therefore the Ching Aling should logically have
    2^8 or 256 octograms. Unfortunately the text of *Mort*
    contradicts this: 'Octogram 8887,' says the wizard
    Cutwell. One mark, then, for the answer 'at least 8887'.
    Two marks for thinking of both answers.

7   They have little doors and windows in them. (*The Light Fantastic*)

8   Hypactic fluid.* (*Equal Rites*)

9   The shy and elusive Standing Stone on a certain moor in the Ramtop Mountains. (*Wyrd Sisters*)

10 The fabled Ice System of Zeret, about which we learn absolutely nothing else. (*The Colour of Magic*)

PITCH
(AS BLACK AS)

---

* Please don't ask what hypactic fluid is.

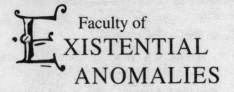

Faculty of EXISTENTIAL ANOMALIES

What is subtly or not so subtly wrong with the following statements?

1   In the Black Oroogu language, the noun meaning 'cabbage' is *n'pong*.

2   'Gods bless this House.'

3   'We're going to do the Rite of AshKente. Right?' (*Reaper Man*)

4   I WAS EXPECTING TO MEET THEE IN PERSEPOLIS. FIVE HUNDRED MILES FROM HERE.

5   'Rincewind . . . had never seen anyone actually killed by magic.' (*Sourcery*)

6   Twoflower, having no sense of smell, was baffled that Rincewind could recognize Ankh-Morpork by its terrible stench the instant they materialized there. (*The Light Fantastic*)

7   The dramatic genius Hwel's best-known play is *Things that Happened on A Midsummer Night*.

8   Twoflower fondly remembered reading all about dragons in *The Octarine Fairy Book* as a child.

9   Death reached out a bony finger and stopped the man's heart.

10 The gates of the Assassins' Guild are always open.

Faculty of Existential Anomalies
ANSWERS

1 Black Oroogu has no nouns – and indeed only one adjective, which is obscene. (*The Colour of Magic*)

2 Magrat's tapestry sampler in *Lords and Ladies* actually reads 'Gods bless this Hosue.'

3 It is dreadful to see people noticing this kind of thing, but *Reaper Man* (at least in its first edition) has AshKente rather than the normal AshkEnte. Similarly, Lavaeolus (*Eric*) was formerly mentioned as Lavaelous (*Pyramids*), the troll Chrysoprase can sometimes appear as Chrysophrase, and that fabled vegetable the wahooni (*Moving Pictures*) later becomes the wahoonie (*The Discworld Companion*). All this is because of quantum; if it seriously worries you we recommend increasing your dosage of dried frog pills.

4 The line in *The Colour of Magic* refers to Psephopololis; the graphic-novel version quoted here changes it to Persepolis, one of the places on Earth (rather than Discworld) about which the legend of Death's appointment is told.

5 Actually Rincewind had seen several of the Seriph's guards nastily killed by magic in an incident fewer than 20 pages previously, but his memory may be short.

6 Earlier in the same book, Twoflower was readily able to detect the smell of frying bacon. But many adventures had followed and perhaps he mislaid his sense of smell in the crowded intervening pages.

7 He abandoned this title as uninteresting and finally called it *The Taming of the Vole*. (*Lords and Ladies*)

8 Perfectly true according to *The Colour of Magic*, but since Twoflower came from the rigidly oppressive Agatean Empire where (see *Interesting Times*) all fictional and most factual reports are forbidden, there is a difficulty. Discworld scholars resolve this by invoking *amnesia auctoris*, or Artistic Licence.*

9 Out of character for Death, who does not himself kill people and indeed is rather sympathetic to them – but here he was evidently still settling into the job. (*The Colour of Magic*)

10 Officially the gates are always open 'because Death is open for business all the time'. Insiders know it was because the hinges rusted centuries ago and no one has ever done anything about it. So it says in *Pyramids*. However . . . by the time of *Men at Arms* someone had evidently found the oil can, since the gates are indeed closed when Carrot and Vimes want to leave after the (you should pardon the expression) crucial confrontation.

* Terry Pratchett has made it clear that there are *no* inconsistencies in the Discworld chronicles. However, out there where the reality is thin, there may be alternative pasts.

Faculty of
'LEY LINES II

Can you think of a Discworld connection
(however tenuous) involving . . .

1   The author Gaston Leroux?

2   The old Sinclair Spectrum computer?

3   Punch & Judy?

4   Aeschylus?

5   The Baker Street Irregulars?

6   Rasputin?

7   The Grateful Dead?

8   John Milton?

9   *Animal Man* and *Doom Patrol*?

10 Mae West?

ANSWERS

1 Leroux wrote the original novel *The Phantom of the Opera* (1911), whose media versions include the famous Lon Chaney silent movie which – as it were – haunts the plot of *Maskerade.** Even Death joins in by wearing a version of Chaney's 'Masque of the Red Death' costume when he calls for the villain.

2 The Spectrum's inbuilt system variable RAMTOP somehow became the name of Discworld's most celebrated and notoriously magical mountain range.

3 The central subject of the short story 'Theatre of Cruelty'. No marks at all for the tenuous argument that 'Neil Gaiman once wrote a novel with Terry, and one of Neil's graphic novels that he did with Dave McKean was called *The Tragical Comedy or Comical Tragedy of MR PUNCH* (1994), and . . .'

4 According to legend, Aeschylus – of Greek tragedy fame – died when an eagle inconsiderately dropped a tortoise on his head. Now see the finale of *Small Gods* . . .

5 The undercover agents of the Ankh-Morpork City Guard in *Maskerade* are the Cable Street Particulars (mentioned also in *Feet of Clay*).

6 The sticky end of Murune, one-time King of Lancre (in *Wyrd Sisters*), as described elsewhere in this invaluable volume (see page 30), is reminiscent of the measures taken by Russian conservatives in 1916 to subtly diminish Rasputin's influence over the Empress Alexandra – including poisoning him, shooting him

---

* Andrew Lloyd Webber? Who's Andrew Lloyd Webber?

twice, tying him up and pushing him through a hole in the ice of the frozen Neva River. He drowned.

7   The Grateful Dead's skull-and-roses motif is recreated in *Soul Music* as Death erupts through rosebeds on the Librarian's 'bike' and continues with a rose between his teeth.

8   Milton was strongly influenced by Terry Pratchett's title *The Light Fantastic* and used the phrase at least twice in his own poems – see *L'Allegro* (1632; 'On the light fantastic toe') and *Comus* (1634; 'In a light fantastic round').

9   Titles of comics worked on by Graham Higgins, the artist on *Mort: A Discworld Big Comic*.

10   Ruby's repartee in *Moving Pictures* was splendidly translated by Detritus: "'Is that the legendary Sceptre of Magma who was King of the Mountain, Smiter of Thousands, Yea, Even Tens of Thousands, Ruler of the Golden River, Master of the Bridges, Delver in Dark Places, Crusher of Many Enemies", he took a deep breath, "in your pocket or are you just glad to see me?"'

Faculty of
ꓒISCOGRAPHY

How should the following phrases be adapted to make more sense in the Common Tongue of Discworld?

1 Greek fire.

2 The Mardi Gras festival in old New Orleans.

3 *Ex Africa semper aliquid novi.*

4 Troy weight.

5 Great Wall of China.

6 'Was this the face that launched a thousand ships, / And burnt the topless towers of Ilium?'

7 All the perfumes of Araby will not sweeten this little hand.

8 'Go, tell the Spartans, thou who passest by, / That here obedient to their laws we lie.'

9 Exquisitely chipped obsidian Aztec knives.

10 Welsh male-voice choirs.

11 Fear the Greeks when they come bearing gifts.

12 'Four and twenty virgins / Came down from Inverness, / And when the ball was over / There were four and twenty less.'

Faculty of Discography
ANSWERS

It's all a question of fine-tuning the geographical references. Approximate answers will do . . .

1 Ephebian fire.

2 Fat Lunchtime in Genua.* (*Witches Abroad*)

3 There is always something new out of Howondaland. (Or Howandaland. Discworld spelling can suffer from the Uncertainty Principle.)

4 Tsort weight. Never accuse an Ankh-Morpork shopkeeper of giving Tsort weight.

5 Very Long Wall Around the Agatean Empire.

6 For Ilium, read 'Tsort' once again.** And half a bonus mark for each of the additional answers: (a) 'yes, it was Elenor of Tsort's face but only metaphorically', and (b) 'no, it was Rincewind when he tripped over the Luggage and dropped the oil lamp'. (*Eric*)

7 All the toilet water in Klatch . . . er, something like that.

8 'Go, tell the Ephebians – ' is as far as that army's sergeant gets when trying to come up with some Famous Last Words as snappy as the memorial to the fallen Spartans at Thermopylae. (*Pyramids*)

9 Exquisitely chipped obsidian Tezumen Empire knives, or thereabouts.

* Where the celebratory fireworks include Klatchian Candles.

** No marks for Pseudopolis, even if Death does say, in *Mort*, IS THIS THE FACE THAT LAUNCHED A THOUSAND SHIPS, / AND BURNED THE TOPLESS TOWERS OF PSEUDOPOLIS? *The Discworld Mapp* confirms that Pseudopolis is nowhere near Tsort . . . Oh, all right, half a mark then.

10 Llamedese malle-voice choirs. Connoisseurs will recognize the double L as not a typographical error but part of the accent. (*Soul Music*)

11 'I fear the Ephebians, especially when they're mad enough to leave bloody great wooden livestock on the doorstep . . .' (*Pyramids*)

12 '. . . vestal virgins / Came down from Heliodeliphilodelphi-boschromenos, / And when the ball was over / There were . . .' From that well known quaffing song *The Ball of Philodelphus*; we are not told the final rhyme. This could be an exciting research project for your holidays! (*Eric*)

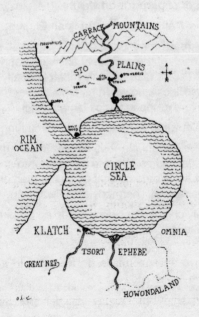

Faculty of
CONTINUUM
ONTOLOGY II

Again, complete or continue the sequences as indicated by the blanks . . .

1 BOGF, BOTD, BOTNS, ——.

2 Chessboard-makers, sellers of onions, ——, people allergic to pewter.

3 Poisoned entrails, ——, ——, tiger's chaudron, baboon hair, mandrake root . . .

4 'Highly enjoyable', 'I would like to eat your foot', 'Your wife is a big hippo', 'Hello, Thinks Mr Purple Cat', ——.

5 Vomit green, unmentionable brown, nicotine yellow, ——.

6 Ashonai, Ebiris, Urshoring, Kvanti, Pythan, N'gurad, ——.

7 1514, 1553, 1557, 1562, ——.

8 Thee legges of an mermade, the hair of an tortoise, the teeth of an fowel, and ——.

9 Chimeran, High Borogravian, Vanglemesht, Sumtri, ——.

10 Morporkian, Vanglemesht, Ephebe, Laotation, ——.

Faculty of Continuum Ontology II
ANSWERS

1   BO101TABCD – section titles in *Pyramids*.

2   Manufacturers of plaster images of small religious
    significance – completing the list of kinds of people
    associated with Rincewind's birth constellation, The
    Small Boring Group of Faint Stars. (*The Light
    Fantastic*)

3   Wholegrain wheat and lentils (too, / In the cauldron
    seethe and stew) – ingredients from a Three Witches'
    Cauldron Scene made slightly more politically correct
    by the determined influence of Magrat. (*Wyrd Sisters*)

4   'Quick! Extra boiling oil!' – the various unexpected
    things that the well known tourist phrase 'Aargh!'
    actually turns out to mean in other languages.
    (*Interesting Times*)

5   Surgical-appliance pink – the universal colours of
    institutional décor, as formalized in *Equal Rites*.

6   Feringomalee – the first seven words of the loosed
    Spell from the Octavo. Rincewind is luckily distracted
    before he can say the (*seven plus one*)th. (*The Colour
    of Magic*)

7   1568 – the dates on which the reign of Queen Grimnir
    the Impaler, Lancre's only royal vampire, began. And
    began again. And again. (*Wyrd Sisters*)

8   The winges of an snake – Broomfog's definition of a
    chimera. (*Sourcery*)

9   Black Oroogu – the languages unsuccessfully tried by
    Rincewind on Twoflower when they first meet. (*The
    Colour of Magic*)

10 'And – several others' – being all Teppic can remember
    of the seven languages he supposedly learned at the
    Assassins' Guild school. (*Pyramids*)

Faculty of
PSEUDONYMY

Give another name for each of the following . . .

1 The Great Wizzard.

2 The Feathered Boa.

3 A Lancre Witch.

4 Fairy Daisy.

5 Boy.

6 Errol.

7 Lucy Tockley.

8 Faust.

9 Bengy 'Lightfoot' Boggis.

10 People helping themselves to musical instruments out of smashed-open shop fronts.

Faculty of Pseudonymy
ANSWERS

1 Rincewind, as he is known to the half-hearted Agatean revolutionaries* in *Interesting Times*.

2 Quezovercoatl, appalling but bijou demon-god of the Tezumen Empire. (*Eric*)

3 Nanny (Gytha) Ogg's nom-de-cookbook in *Maskerade*.

4 Granny Weatherwax, issued with an unconvincing flower-fairy identity by Magrat. (*Witches Abroad*)

5 Mort in *Mort*.

6 Goodboy Bindle Featherstone of Quirm, swamp dragon extraordinaire and suspected whittle. (*Guards! Guards!*)

7 Diamanda. (*Lords and Ladies*)

8 Eric – as visibly corrected on the cover of *Eric*.

9 Brother Fingers. (*Guards! Guards!*)

10 Luters. (*The Light Fantastic*)

* 'Slight Unpleasantness To Oppressors When Convenient!'

Faculty of
CLAIRAUDIENCE III

Once again, who or what, on these various occasions, is speaking, shouting, shrieking, etc.?

1   Kwesta!? Maladetta!!

2   Meeeyisss Magraaaaat Garrrrrli-ck!

3   Ee cuns uk ere um-imes an awks oo ugg.

4   Shometimes we jusht have to take rishks.

5   A – – – –ing wizard. I *hate* – – – –ing wizards!

6   Rrrrighttt . . . Iiiinnn tthhatttt cccasseee –

7   *The death of all wizardry is at hand.*

8   I EXPECT YOU'D LIKE A LITTLE TIME AWAY FROM THE UNIVERSITY, EH?

9   Where The Gate Is, There Am I Also . . .

10 Shutuphereshecomes.

Faculty of Clairaudience III
ANSWERS

1 Agnes/Perdita imitating Christine's singing voice all too accurately. (*Maskerade*)

2 Young Shawn making a formal announcement. (*Lords and Ladies*)

3 The gargoyle Cornice-overlooking-Broadway, reminiscing about Carrot. (*Men at Arms*)

4 Cohen the Barbarian. (*The Light Fantastic*)

5 An Ankh-Morporkian thief apparently called Pilgarlic. (*Mort*) Needless to say, the reply is: 'You shouldn't – – – – them, then.'

6 Granny Weatherwax, 'slightly blurred from hitting an absolutely immovable object'. (*Equal Rites*)

7 The Archchancellor's Hat. (*Sourcery*)

8 Ridcully dropping subtle hints to the Bursar. (*Lords and Ladies*)

9 Osric, or Oswald, or Osbert, according to Achmed the Mad's *Necrotelecomnicon*. (*Moving Pictures*)

10 Ysabell to Mort, speaking of Queen Keli. (*Mort*)

Faculty of PRIMACY

Where in our author's works do we first meet or hear about . . .

1 The ancient Agatean emperor, One Sun Mirror?

2 Alberto Malich, Founder of Unseen University?

3 Roof gargoyles' ability to move around?

4 Hogswatchnight?

5 Swamp dragons (*Draconis vulgaris*)?

6 The dread name of Weatherwax?

7 The Counterweight Continent's vizier, Nine Turning Mirrors?

8 The poisonous effects of quicksilver fumes as an occupational hazard of magic-users?

9 A loud imprecation that, owing to the presence of magic, takes on living form?

10 The Midgard Serpent?

11 Captain Carrot?

12 The archetypal folk-tune 'Mrs Widgery's Lodger'?

Faculty of Primacy
ANSWERS

1 A footnote in *Mort*.

2 *Equal Rites*.

3 *The Light Fantastic*.

4 *The Dark Side of the Sun* . . . which, yes, is a science-
fiction novel not involving any actual Discworld. Them's
the breaks. It also introduces the red-letter days of
Soul Cake Friday (Tuesday or Thursday on Discworld)
and the Eve of Small Gods.

5 *The Colour of Magic*.

6 *The Light Fantastic* – not Granny but Galder
Weatherwax, current Chancellor of Unseen University.

7 *The Colour of Magic*.

8 *The Colour of Magic*.

9 *Mort*. (Did you say *Reaper Man*? Be honest.)

10 *The Colour of Magic* – the world-circling dragon
reported in Tethis's account of his space journey to
Discworld.

11 *Men at Arms* . . . but only at the end of this book does
he actually become Captain.

12 *Strata*.

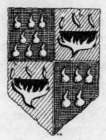

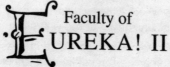

Faculty of EUREKA! II

Once again, what's the first Discworld book
to feature each of the following ideas,
inventions and processes?

1   In-flight refuelling.

2   Hypnopaedia.

3   Escalators.

4   Extraction of uranium from pitchblende.

5   The stuffed olive.

6   Filofaxes.

7   A glider built from silk and bamboo.

8   Bumper stickers.

9   The flight recorder.

10 The concept of filterable viruses.

Faculty of Eureka! II
ANSWERS

1 *Wyrd Sisters* – where it's Granny Weatherwax's broomstick that (in a suicidal manoeuvre) is topped up with magic while proceeding at a great height.

2 *Small Gods* – invented by Didactylos to pump learning into the impatient Prince of Tsort while he slept.

3 *Sourcery* – where Rincewind's magically created escalator is, uniquely, floored with alligator skin.

4 *Moving Pictures* – strongly hinted, at least, when Silverfish the alchemist cooks up a ton of ore to create the silvery metal that he'd hoped would open 'the way to a new, clear future' but which ends up being dubbed Uselessium.

5 *Pyramids* – invented by Dil the embalmer (or Dil the Pickler) as foundation of a possible new career.

6 *Sourcery* offers the suspiciously similar Fullomyth.

7 *The Colour of Magic* – one of the rare creations of Goldeneyes Silverhand Dactylos which didn't earn him a horrid mutilation.

8 *Guards! Guards!* – on Lady Ramkin's carriage, 'Whinny If You Love Dragons'.*

9 *Wyrd Sisters* – a small black raven trained by Goodie Whemper.

10 *Pyramids* – a problem caused 'by something so small it can't be detected in any way whatsoever', bluffs the doctor, and adds with growing confidence, 'It's probably a walrus.'

---

* Another example of the genre appears in *Moving Pictures*: 'Ankh-Morpork – Loathe It or Leave It'.

Faculty of 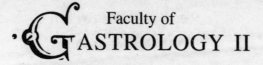GASTROLOGY II

A second bite at this particular cherry . . .

1 What type of exotic delicacy, served in a strangely wrought box of compressed fibres, is a Klatchian Hots?

2 What substance is detectable in a sufficiently detailed tattoo showing that naughty position, the Congress of The Friendly Dog and the Two Small Biscuits?

3 What is supplied instead of beer owing to the provider Skrp's reading difficulties?

4 What nice little nibble is enjoyed after a good meal of *Petit porc rôti avec pommes de terre nouvelles et légumes du jour et bière glacée avec figment de l'imagination*?

5 What is the vegetarian option in Gimlet's dwarf delicatessen?

6 A random spray of magic turned one of the Seriph's palace walls into what?

7 Complete this food-related comparison: 'The Ramkins were more highly bred than . . .'

8 Vengeful supernatural forces caused what to be over-salted?

9 What was vaguely bivalvular and contained a small slip of paper inscribed: 'Many, many apologies.'?

10 There was something purple in there and it had at least ten legs – what kind of stew was this?

ANSWERS

1   A takeaway pizza, probably with anchovies or salami.
    Sergeant Colon's Tips for Gourmets #168: 'The cheese
    goes all manky when it gets cold.' (*Guards! Guards!*)

2   Yoghurt. (*Pyramids*)

3   Merckle and Stingbat's Very Famous Brown Sauce.
    Skrp and the Patrician's other trained rats had never
    really got the hang of reading the labels. (*Guards!
    Guards!*)

4   Three desert centipedes (*Chilopoda aridius*), fancied
    by St Ungulant. (*Small Gods*)

5   Soya rat. (*Men at Arms*) We'll allow a mark for 'Cream-
    cheese rat' – found on Gimlet's menu in the same book
    – even though this might conceivably be cream cheese
    and rat.

6   Arsenic meringue. Not lime custard, which is what a
    ceiling got turned into. (*Sourcery*)

7   A hilltop bakery. (*Men at Arms*)

8   Duke Felmet's porridge . . . the supernatural force
    being the ghost of his victim King Verence I. (*Wyrd
    Sisters*)

9   The fortune cookie served to Rincewind in an Agatean
    inn, expressing regret that his immediate future would
    involve being coshed into unconsciousness.
    (*Interesting Times*)

10 Fish stew* at Borgle's in Holy Wood, compounded on
    the principle that, if you find it in water, it's a fish.
    (*Moving Pictures*)

---

* Also known as primal soup.

Faculty of
RHETORICAL FLORA

Identify the subjects of these similes and metaphors . . .

1 A piece of rubbish covered with the diseased secretions of a dying mollusc.

2 Its eyes were the size of very large eyes.

3 Nothing more than a comma on the page of History.

4 As efficient a killer as a psychotic mongoose.

5 As sharp as goblin's teeth in the silver light.

6 Made Gormenghast look like a toolshed on a railway allotment.

7 Had the same prospects of long-term employment as a pogo stick tester in a minefield.

8 An ice-blue sinewave arcing through the dark dimensions.

9 Like a kzak fruit through a short grandmother.

10 Like plum jam, or possibly blackberry preserve.

11 Like the unexpected limbo dancer under the lavatory door of Life.

12 A martlebury full of mizzensails.

Faculty of Rhetorical Flora
ANSWERS

1　Ankh-Morpork! Pearl of cities! (*The Light Fantastic*)

2　The summoned dragon (*Draco nobilis*) in *Guards! Guards!*

3　Coin's great-grandfather. (*Sourcery*, first paragraph)

4　Bentzen, captain of Duke Felmet's personal bodyguard. (*Wyrd Sisters*)

5　Two mountains of the Ramtops between which our hero flies in *Mort*.

6　Unseen University. (*Equal Rites*)

7　The senior wizard of Unseen University. (*Moving Pictures*)

8　How Rincewind's and Twoflower's return from an astral trip to the house of Death was specifically not described. (*The Light Fantastic*)

9　Queen Keli's nomadic ancestor, predicting how rapidly his men would penetrate Sto Lat's city defences. (*Mort*)

10　Night spreading across the Disc. (*Sourcery*)

11　How an unwanted but persistent thought arrived in Esk's mind – i.e., that she couldn't remain a hidden stowaway for ever but would need to relieve herself . . . (*Equal Rites*)

12　'I'faith, nuncle, thou't more full of questions than a martlebury is of mizzensails' – the Fool of the Lancre Court hastily lapsing into character after unthinkingly talking solid sense. (*Wyrd Sisters*)

Faculty of MORPHIC RESONANCE

Only connect – via Discworld if neither member of a pair is itself Discworldish . . .

1. The Eightfold Seal of Stasis and Rincewind's sock.

2. Sir Isaac Newton and hatters.

3. Sir Francis Drake and Ankh-Morpork civil defence.

4. Granny Whitlow and Black Aliss.

5. Jacqueline Susann and Holy Wood.

6. Death and P.C. Wren.

7. Sexual aspiration and false moustaches.

8. Solomon and the Seriph of Al Khali.

9. Sodom and Pseudopolis.

10. Victor Hugo and the Opera House.

Faculty of Morphic Resonance
ANSWERS

1 Half a brick. The Eightfold Seal of Stasis is regarded by wizards 'to have all the stopping power of a well aimed halfbrick' . . . which, in a sock, is Rincewind's chosen weapon against the invincible power of the Sourcerer.

2 The mercury fumes which account for certain health problems of alchemists (see *Moving Pictures*) were historically responsible for the notorious madness of hatters and, it is believed, the loony phases of Sir Isaac Newton – who at one stage made alchemical experiments with boiling mercury.

3 Drake's drum. According to legend, a similar drum in the Patrician's Palace will beat of its own accord if an enemy fleet sails up the Ankh. Of course it would need to be a fleet of rust- and rot-proof dredgers . . . (*Soul Music*)

4 Both lived in gingerbread cottages. It was once quite a fad, 'the Confectionery School of Architecture'. (*The Light Fantastic*)

5 *Valley of the Trolls.* (*Moving Pictures*)

6 P.C. Wren's best-selling series of Foreign Legion novels began with *Beau Geste* (1924); the Klatchian Foreign Legion has a tip of the hat to Wren when Death joins to forget, proves apathetic, and becomes known as Beau Nidle. (*Soul Music*)

7 After Granny Ogg drew facial hair on the pictures in the deeply inexperienced King of Lancre's *Sexe Manuale*, he was heard enquiring where he could get a couple of false moustaches . . . (*Maskerade*)

8 In *Sourcery*, the Seriph's most improbable simile of praise for Conina – that her hair is like a flock of goats – is lifted straight from the Biblical *Song of Solomon*.

9 The Marquis de Sade's nasty book *The 120 Days of Sodom* (1785) is echoed in Discworld's *130 Days of Pseudopolis*. Ptraci in *Pyramids* is unimpressed by a scene from this work: 'It's physically impossible.'

10 The musical *Miserable Les*. (*Maskerade*)

Faculty of
EGREGIOSITY III

Yet again your powers of detecting the Odd One
Out in each set are challenged. Which is it?

1   *Diseases of the Dragon, The Interestinge and Curious
    Adventures of Cohen the Barbarian, Achmed the I Just
    Get These Headaches's Book of Humorous Cat Stories,
    Dictionary of Eye-Watering Words, Jane's All the
    World's Siege Weapons.*

2   *Diseases of the Dragon, What I Did on My Holidays, The
    Joye of Snacks, The Laws and Ordinances of The Cities
    of Ankh and Morpork, Meditations.*

3   *Diseases of the Dragon, Blert Wheedown's Guitar
    Primer, The Servant, The Bumper Fun Grimoire, Inne
    Juste 7 Dayes I Will Make You a Barbearian Hero!*

4   The Vase of Tulips, The Celestial Parsnip, The Cow of
    Heaven, The Pool of Night, The Flying Moose, The
    Knotted String.

5   Ear Wilt, Octarine Garget, Abated Heel, Wooden Udder.

6   Bad Ass, Razorback, Slippery Hollow, Slice, Scrote.

7   Ankhstones, Irexes, Roseattes, Spircles, Ultramarines.

8   Brotherhood of the Hoodwink, Venerable Council of
    Seers, Illuminated Mages of the Unbroken Circle,
    Brothers of the Order of Midnight, Illuminated and
    Ancient Brethren of Ee.

9   Berilia, Cubal, Jerakeen, Tubul, Great T'phon.

10 Sheaf of Plenty, Reaping Hook of Justice, Honeycomb of
    Increase, Staff of Ossory, Cabbage of Vegetative
    Increase, Scapula of Hygiene.

ANSWERS

1 The Cohen title is a click (see *Moving Pictures*); the others are books.

2 All but the *Laws and Ordinances* were written by contemporary Discworld characters – respectively, Lady Ramkin, Twoflower, Nanny Ogg and Didactylos.

3 Lord Vetinari's *The Servant* is alone in being an unpublished work.

4 All are Discworld constellations except The Pool of Night, which is a Caroc card.

5 All are diseases of Ramtop Mountains goats except Abated Heel, which afflicts swamp dragons.

6 No, not more diseases but towns and villages – all in the Kingdom of Lancre except for Scrote.

7 All are Discworld jewels except Irexes, an Ephebian philosopher.

8 All are wizardly orders at Unseen University, except the Brethren of Ee.

9 Four names are those of the huge elephants that support the Discworld; the fifth name, Cubal, is an interpolated Ephebian fire-god.

10 All are parts of the divine paraphernalia of the King of Djelibeybi in *Pyramids*, except the Staff of Ossory, relating to a prophet of Om in *Small Gods*.

Faculty of
·DISCOGRAPHY II

Identify these places and features of the Discworld
landscape, past and present . . .

1 A land whose sinking into the ocean several thousand
   years ago ranked as the multiverse's most embarrassing
   continental catastrophe.

2 Region where, by all the logic of morphic resonance, one
   should be able to find a popular American brand of
   chocolate.

3 Small city with a floral clock, where, 150 or so years ago,
   a man was killed by a freak shower of goulash.

4 Has a world-famous cuisine of pasta, tomatoes, olive oil
   and seafood.

5 Tasty-sounding city where Lord McSweeney arranged for
   the execution of 30 rebels who weren't.

6 Location of the universally famous Place Where the Sun
   Does Not Shine.

7 City where gourmet delight can famously be conjured up
   from the squeezings of a handful of mud, a few dead
   leaves and a pinch or two of herbs.

8 Inverted mountain sustained by being in a region of high residual magic.

9 Klatchian city with a vaguely criminal sound, one of whose rulers suffered from an irritating variant of the King Midas syndrome.

10 Once discovered by, among others, Abraxas of Ephebe and Truckle of the Silver Horde.

11 The problem with 'Kingdom of the Sun' as a postal address for the royal family of Djelibeybi.

12 Islands discovered (though the natives didn't think of it that way) by Llamedos Jones, missionary of Strict Druidism.

Faculty of Discography II
ANSWERS

1 The continent of Ku, which took 30 years to subside . . . so the Kuians spent a lot of this period wading around and suffering a humiliating lack of drama. (*Eric*)

2 Hersheba.*

3 Quirm. The goulash report appeared in Miss Flitworth's *Farmer's Almanac and Seed Catalogue*, so of course it must be true. (*Reaper Man*)

4 Brindisi, ostensible home and culinary bane of Señor Enrico Basilica. (*Maskerade*)

5 Sum Dim, in the Agatean Empire. Since there had definitely been no revolutionary Red Army cadre there, the executions ensured that one would now emerge. (*Interesting Times*)

6 Slice, in the Kingdom of Lancre. Population: seven.

7 Genua, whose best cooks scorned all that 'pork and beef and lamb and rubbish for them that never tasted anything better'. (*Witches Abroad*)

---

* Try saying it out loud. Louder! Louder! Stressing different syllables! Louder still! If you're reading this on public transport, other people should be getting interested by now.

8 The Wyrmberg, where the strong magical ambience allows the conjuring of dragons and has even crept into people's names: K!sdra, Lio!rt, M!Caffrey Sp!!f, etc. (*The Colour of Magic*)

9 Al-Ybi, whose Seriph was cursed by a somewhat dyslexic deity so that for some days everything he touched turned into Glod, a dwarf who resented this repeated duplication. (*Witches Abroad*)

10 The Lost City of Ee – thought to lie in the Great Nef, but may well move around a bit. (*Interesting Times*)

11 There are at least 11 Kingdoms of the Sun on the Disc, according to Teppic's sarky housemaster at the Assassins' school. (*Pyramids*)

12 The Brown Islands, one of which to this day upholds the Llamedos traditions of choral singing, football with a non-round ball, and rain. (*The Discworld Mapp*)

Faculty of
OOK

A clutch of easyish ones with a common theme . . .
just name what's being talked about in each case.

1 Half of this was a charred lump.

2 Rincewind briefly inhabited it.

3 Was used without success in an attempt to end a noisy haunting.

4 Revealed the secrets of double finessing.

5 Was hurled with lethal force owing to a problem with metaphor.

6 They were entirely blank.

7 Enabled the correct identification of Gods.

8 Revealed that the sun was the Eye of Yay, toiling across the sky each day in His endless search for His toenails.

9 Where one can find out about the three London Underground stations they never dare show on public maps.

10 Dealt with activities rather late in the morning.

ANSWERS

'Oook' of course means Librarianship, so naturally the questions all involve books. Or booklike things.

1   *The Summoning of Dragons* by Tubal de Malachite. (*Guards! Guards!*)

2   The Octavo. (*The Light Fantastic*)

3   Humptemper's *Names of the Ants*, in conjunction with a candle and the bell Old Tom: exorcism by bell, book and candle. (*Eric*)

4   Twoflower's prized copy of *Nosehinger on the Laws of Contract*, as in contract bridge. (*The Light Fantastic*)

5   *The Laws and Ordinances of The Cities of Ankh and Morpork*: 'Throw the book at him, Carrot,' said Captain Vimes incautiously. (*Guards! Guards!*)

6   Death's self-writing autobiographies of people who had yet to be born. (*Mort*)

7   *Ego-Video Liber Deorum*, the 'I-Spy Book of Gods', by Koomi of Smale. (*Small Gods*)

8   *The Book of Staying in The Pit*. (*Pyramids*)

9   The deluxe, spiderskin-bound Fullomyth. (*Sourcery*)

10 *The Book of Going Forth Around Elevenish*. (*The Light Fantastic*)

Faculty of **M**ORPHIC RESONANCE II

Again, work out a half-way convincing connection between the following pairs, dragging in Discworld if it's not there already . . .

1 Laurel & Hardy and the Marx Brothers.

2 Robert Browning's 'Childe Roland to the Dark Tower Came' and a Hero's challenge in Ankh-Morpork.

3 Dylan Thomas and rain-drenched stone circles.

4 Plato's cave and Deformed Rabbit.

5 Earthquakes and the resograph.

6 The showman P.T. Barnum and Rincewind.

7 Homer's seafarer who was tired of the sea, and Music With Rocks In.

8 William Pitt the Younger (Prime Minister 1783–1801 and 1804–1806) and Windle Poons – apart from the initials, that is.

9 Magrat and the ballad of Tam Lin.

10 Moules (as defined in the *Dictionary of Eye-Watering Words*) and Zeno of Elea.

ANSWERS

1 Thanks to narrative resonance, Hwel the playwright is baffled to find himself inspired in successive paragraphs with comic dialogue reminiscent of both: first a dose of Groucho-style double-talk and then 'Thys is amain Dainty Messe youe have got me into, Stanleigh . . .' (*Wyrd Sisters*)

2 The note of challenge, both at the door of the Dark Tower and to the Ankh-Morpork dragon in *Guards! Guards!*, is sounded on a slug-horn.* The original word means battle-cry, as in 'slogan': Terry Pratchett is having a little quiet fun with the fact that the poets Chatterton and Browning thought it meant the sort of horn you blow.

3 Dylan Thomas's mythic Welsh village of *Under Milk Wood* is called Llareggub;** Discworld's land of rain and stone circles is Llamedos; both names have a special ring when pronounced backwards. (*Soul Music*)

4 Plato had this famous analogy of life as being like a cave in which we see only shadows of the reality outside. In accordance with the universal Law of Running Gags, Didactylos's version adds a request to the Unseen for a particular shadow-picture: 'Go on, do Deformed Rabbit . . . it's my favourite.' (*Small Gods*)

5 The resograph, or reality-disturbance meter, in *Moving Pictures* is actually based on an ancient Chinese design of crude seismograph . . . and its inventor 'Numbers' Riktor does vaguely recall the Richter scale of earthquake intensity.

---

* Nobby of the City Watch: 'It must have been a bloody big slug.'

** A bowdlerized spelling is Llaregyb; the Welsh 'y' is pronounced as 'u', so it comes to the same thing.

6   The showman P.T. Barnum's famous saying, 'There's a sucker born every minute', is echoed by Rincewind in *Interesting Times*. 'Make Considerable Sacrifice For The Common Good,' says a slogan-happy revolutionary, to which Rincewind replies, '"There's One Born Every Minute."'

7   The *Odyssey* tells of a weary seafarer who meant to walk inland with an oar over his shoulder until he reached a place where *no one would recognize what he was carrying* – and there he'd settle down at last. Cliff the drummer in *Soul Music* plans exactly the same trick with his musical kit, which consists of a set of rocks . . .

8   Pitt's supposed last words were, 'I think I could eat one of Bellamy's veal pies.' Poons's last living words were, strangely enough, 'What I could do with right now is one of Mr Dibbler's famous meat pies – '

9   Magrat Garlick in *Lords and Ladies* finds herself in the position of Fair Janet who lost her Tam Lin, and has clearly read the old ballad: 'I remember a folksong about a situation just like this . . . This girl had her fiancé stolen by the Queen of the Elves and she didn't hang around whining, she jolly well . . . went and rescued him.'

10 Yes, of course it was on the tip of your tongue. Zeno of Elea (495–435 BC) boggled Greek philosophers with mischievous paradoxes 'proving' that, for example, an arrow in flight cannot move and that the notorious sprinter Achilles would never be able to overtake a tortoise. Discworld's Xeno of Ephebe, being more practical, set up his Axiom Testing Station (CAUTION – UNRESOLVED POSTULATES) to demonstrate that it is impossible for an arrow in flight to overtake a tortoise. Result: a lot of tortoises on sticks. Clearly the whole experimental procedure is a game of skill and dexterity involving tortoises – which is the *Dictionary of Eye-Watering Words*'s definition of 'moules'. (*Pyramids, Guards! Guards!*)

Faculty of
CONTINUUM
ONTOLOGY III

Yet again, complete or continue the sequences as indicated by the blanks . . .

1 'Silence, Books must be returned no later than the last date shown, ——.'

2 Up, down, sideways, sex appeal, ——.

3 Rats, ants, bedbugs, gargoyles, ——.

4 Half man, ——, half jaguar, half serpent, half scorpion, half mad.

5 Talking Vase, Jade Head, ——, Diamond Coffin, Singing Sword.

6 Ill-preparedness, Carelessness, Lack of concentration, Poor maintenance of tools, and ——.

7 Wonderful, marvellous, fantastic, glamorous, ——, ——.

8 Cut-price turrets, ——, buttresses, crenellations, gargoyles, towers, courtyards, keeps, dungeons.

9 Ossory, Fruni, Cena, Wallspur, Abbys, Hashimi, ——.

10 Shirt, mail, chain; helmet, iron and copper; breastplate, iron; ——.

ANSWERS

1 'Do not interfere with the nature of causality' – the third of the three rules of the Librarians of Time and Space. (*Guards! Guards!*)

2 Peppermint – these are the five 'flavours' of resons or reality fragments into which the thaum, once thought the ultimate, indivisible unit of magic, has been split by High Energy Magic experiments. Not in the least reminiscent of real-world quarks: up, down, strange (or sideways), charmed, top (or truth) and bottom (or beauty). (*Lords and Ladies*)

3 Cockroaches – these were the successive waves of inhabitants fleeing Unseen University in its hour of greatest peril. Only wizards lacked the basic common sense to run for it. (*Sourcery*)

4 Half chicken – these are the attributes of the demon Quezovercoatl, adding up to a total of three homicidal maniacs. It's a good thing he's only six inches high, really. (*Eric*)

5 The secret of how silk is made – this list is the series of guesses by Six Beneficent Winds regarding exactly what the Silver Horde intends to steal from the Empire. (*Interesting Times*)

6 Over-confidence – these are the inner enemies which, according to the teacher, dog Assassins' footsteps. (*Pyramids*)

7 Enchanting, terrific – these are the misleading attributes of elves (a bad lot) listed in *Lords and Ladies*.

8   Bargain basements complete this list of the noteworthy architectural features of Lancre Castle. (*Wyrd Sisters*)

9   Ishkible completes the list of the Seven Prophets of the Omnian Church. (*Small Gods*)

10 Truncheon, oak – the items listed are the standard issue to new Night Watch constables. (*Men at Arms*)

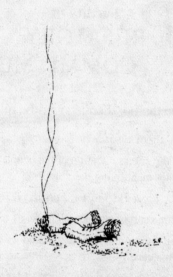

Faculty of
PREFATORY
COMMITMENT

Spot the theme, then answer the questions.

1 Who knew about L-space?

2 What was the communication of the people who were repaid by not mentioning their names?

3 Whence the *Liber Paginarum Fulvarum*?

4 Where is the shortest of them all?

5 What is the traditional curse associated with a debatable or borderline case?

6 When and where came the imaginative leap from little rattly wheels to lots of little legs?

7 Where can you find an example of Lewis Carroll's rule of fulsomeness, 'What I tell you three times is true'?

8 Who provoked the response: 'Deary deary me'?

9 What permission was granted to disappointed map connoisseurs?

10 Where does football person Bruce Grobelaar come into all this?

ANSWERS

We are talking about literary dedication here. That is, dedications.

1   Mike Harrison, Mary Gentle, Neil Gaiman and others. (*Guards! Guards!*)

2   'That opera was stranger than I could imagine.' (*Maskerade*)

3   Allegedly loaned by Neil Gaiman. (*Equal Rites*)

4   In *Mort*: 'To Rhianna' – Rhianna being Terry and Lyn Pratchett's daughter.

5   'May You Live In Interesting Times' – debatable since, although this bit occupies the normal dedication slot in *Interesting Times*, it isn't exactly a dedication – more of an epigraph. (Those who wish to argue the point furiously get no mark for this question. Yes, we can be petty.)

6   'Many years ago . . . in Bath', when Terry Pratchett saw a very large American lady struggling with a huge wheeled suitcase and the Luggage sprang fully armed from his brow – which wasn't comfortable. (*Sourcery*)

7   The parodic dedication of *Moving Pictures*: 'Thank you. Thank you. Thank you . . .'

8   Those who 'deluged the author with their version of the words of "The Hedgehog Song" '. (*Witches Abroad*)

9   'Please feel free to draw your own.' (*Sourcery* again)

10 Graham Higgins's additional dedication in the *Mort* graphic novel.

Faculty of
EXTERNAL
STUDIES

A set of slightly more outward-looking questions
. . . but all of them share a Discworld angle.

1   Who was the king of fantasy, and what collection came
   after him?

2   What strikes you as Discworldly about the first issue of
   Neil Gaiman's *Sandman* comic?

3   Which would-be-humorous fantasy novel goes on about a
   box made from insipid wormwood?

4   Which villain in Alan Garner's *The Weirdstone of
   Brisingamen* shares a name with a past ruler of Lancre?

5   You've heard of *Howondaland Smith, Balgrog Hunter*,
   but where would you find *Alabama Smith and the Jewels
   of Fate*?

6   Which character in Thomas Pynchon's *The Crying of Lot
   49* rings an interesting bell?

7   If Scrote is Nürnberg, then Pseudopolis is . . . ?

8   The pointy-eared wizard on the back cover of British
   editions of *Equal Rites* is a caricature of . . . whom?*

9   How does sf author Gene Wolfe link *Pyramids* with
   Small Gods?

10 Why do you know nothing whatever about the Discworld
   novels called *Unclear Physics* and *Imperial Wizard*?

---

* We apologize to unfortunates on the cover of whose edition of
Equal Rites this character is not visible. This is why there aren't pages
and pages of questions about jacket artwork . . .

Faculty of External Studies

ANSWERS

1   J.R.R. Tolkien was the king, according to the title of
    After the King: Stories in Honour of J.R.R. Tolkien
    (1992), edited by Martin H. Greenberg. It saw the first
    publication of the Discworld short story 'Troll Bridge'.

2   There is this grimoire called the *Paginarum Fulvarum* . . .*

3   *Dirty Work* (1993) by Dan McGirt – compare the
    Discworld's 'sapient pearwood'. Insipid wormwood
    differs chiefly in being very unfunny.

4   Alan Garner's Grimnir; Queen Grimnir the Impaler of
    Lancre. *Pedantry alert:* This is a very, very old name.
    Grimnir, 'The Grim One', is used as an alias by Odin in
    the Icelandic *Elder Edda*.

5   It's a computer game mentioned in *Only You Can Save
    Mankind* . . . an entirely different novel series, yes, but
    still by that man Pratchett.

---

*   And in a much later *Sandman* episode there's a visit to the Royal
Society – formerly the Invisible College, nudge nudge – featuring the
deeply repulsive dissection of an unfortunate orang-utan. You don't
suppose . . . ? Another Gaiman-scripted graphic novel, *The Books of
Magic* (1990), manages to contort its plot so that a character can
plausibly report: 'A *thousand* elephants . . .'

6   Genghis Cohen – reminding us that Cohen the
    Barbarian promoted himself to Ghenghiz Cohen in
    Interesting Times. Other points of similarity to
    Pynchon's 'most eminent philatelist in the LA area' are
    difficult to detect. The Watch suspects that well known
    offender the Long Arm of Cohencidence.*

7   Seville. In Discworld opera, *Die Meistersinger von
    Nürnberg* becomes *Die Meistersinger von Scrote* and
    The Barber of Seville becomes *The Barber of
    Pseudopolis*. (*Maskerade*)

8   Josh Kirby, the artist responsible for innumerable
    British Discworld jackets. Well, innumerable in the Troll
    counting system.

9   The third section title in *Pyramids*, 'The Book of the
    New Son', echoes Wolfe's superb sf sequence *The
    Book of the New Sun* (1980-83). Wolfe's hero is a
    torturer called Severian who can forget nothing and
    who rises to supreme political and theological power –
    like Brutha in *Small Gods*. (As another nudge in the
    same Discworld book, St Ungulant's first name is
    Sevrian.)

10 *Unclear Physics* was a temporary working title for what
    eventually appeared as *Interesting Times*. (One reason
    for its non-use was that this story was a bit short of,
    well, unclear physics; the title may yet resurface in
    some more appropriate context of High Energy Magic.)
    Imperial Wizard was another tentative title for the same
    book. Out there in the dim wits of Usenet there is a
    vast body of misinformation about *Unclear Physics* and
    the apocryphal Missing Chapter of one Discworld
    novel. You really do not wish to know any of this.

---

* I think Terry Pratchett would like to distance himself from this even
further than from the rest of the book. Me too.

Faculty of
LOGOPODY

Another 'theme' paper that gets to the bottom of
things . . .

1   What was the Creator's intended pizza recipe?

2   What is the old Ankh-Morporkian civic anthem?

3   On what basis do Ankh-Morpork citizens claim the river
    water is incredibly pure?

4   How much magic is required – according to the standard
    definition – to materialize one small white pigeon or three
    normal-sized billiard balls?

5   What else is Nature said to abhor besides vacuums and
    ships called the *Marie Celeste*?*

6   The selfish little bastard will do anything rather than let
    go of *what*?

7   What's so odd about the calendar of the Theocracy of
    Muntab?

* Known in our own world as the *Mary Celeste*.

8 What is the universal magical significance of half a jar of elderly mayonnaise, a piece of very old cheese, and a tomato with white mould growing on it?

9 In the Guild of Merchants' famous survey of tradespeople in the dock areas of Morpork, how many women gave their profession as 'seamstress'?

10 Certain important technical processes (unconnected for once with mining) are explained to dwarfs when they reach puberty – at about what age?

11 Who built the famous Collapsed Tower of Quirm?

12 What high-order elementary particles travel faster not only than Discworld light (which almost anything can do) but than ordinary light?

Faculty of Logopody
ANSWERS

All these questions are answered somewhere in the small print of the Discworld novels' famous footnotes.*

1   Cheese and pepperoni with a few black olives. The additional mountains and seas that resulted in Discworld were 'added out of last-minute enthusiasm, as so often happens'. (*Mort*)

2   'We Can Rule You Wholesale.' (*Moving Pictures*)

3   Anything that has passed through so many kidneys has to be very pure indeed. (*Sourcery*)

4   One Thaum. (*The Light Fantastic*)

5   The chuck keys for electric drills. (*Pyramids*)

6   Its skin – the little bastard being the vermine, whose fur is much prized. (*Sourcery*)

7   This calendar counts *down*, not up. 'No one knows why, but it might not be a good idea to hang around and find out.' (*Wyrd Sisters*)

8   The contents of any larder raided furtively in the middle of the night . . . no matter what its contents might be by daylight. (*Mort*)

9   987 – but an approximate answer will do. Or even a wildly wrong one, provided you remembered that the same survey found just two needles. (*Men at Arms*)

10 55 . . . any answer within about ten years is fine. (*Guards! Guards!*)

---

*   Which are funnier than this one.

11 Bloody Stupid Johnson. Of course. Lesser architects would confine themselves to mere *leaning* towers . . . (*Maskerade*)

12 Kingons and queons, the postulated exchange particles which *instantly* transfer the royal succession to the next heir upon the death of a king or queen. Ly Tin Wheedle speculated that these tachyonic particles could be used to send messages, by carefully torturing a small king in order to modulate the signal. (*Mort*)

Faculty of
SYNECDOCHE

Complete the following well known (or occasionally bloody obscure) phrases or sayings, at least approximately . . .

1   Remember, A Dragon is For Life . . .

2   Do not meddle in the affairs of wizards, because . . .

3   It doesn't say it anywhere . . .

4   It is said that if danger ever threatens the city . . .

5   It wasn't blood in general he couldn't stand the sight of . . .

6   I'd like to know if I could compare you to . . .

7   Lord of Sto Lat, Protector of the Eight Protectorates, and . . .

8   If you can find an ant on Hogswatch Day . . .

9   You know what *really* gets me down is the way that in opera everyone takes . . .

10 Hex 'em till they glow . . .

11 That's the last time the universe is going to . . .

12 When a man is tired of Ankh-Morpork . . .

Faculty of Synecdoche
ANSWERS

1 . . . Not Just for Hogswatchnight. (Motto of the
Sunshine Sanctuary for Sick Dragons in Morphic
Street, Ankh-Morpork – in various books.

2 . . . a refusal often offends. (*Mort*) Not to be confused
with: 'Do not meddle in the affairs of wizards,
especially simian ones. They're not all that subtle.'
(*Lords and Ladies*)

3 . . . it says it everywhere. (That women can't be
wizards – *Equal Rites*.)

4 . . . they will run away. (The heraldic hippos on Ankh-
Morpork's Brass Bridge – *Pyramids*.)

5 . . . it was just his blood in particular that was so
upsetting. (Rincewind's, inevitably – *Sourcery*.)

6 . . . a summer's day. Because, well, June 12th was
quite nice . . . (The Fool suavely chatting up Magrat in
Wyrd Sisters.)

7 . . . Empress of the Long Thin Debated Piece
Hubwards of Sto Kerrig. (*Mort*)

8 . . . it will be very mild for the rest of the winter. (*Equal
Rites*)

9 . . . such a *long!!!!!* . . . time!!!!! . . . to!!!!! . . . argh . . .
argh . . . argh . . . (The villain's artistic dying speech, or
aria, in *Maskerade*.)

10 . . . then curse them in the dark. (*Sourcery*)

11 . . . trick Rincewi – (Quoth Rincewind, scant
nanoseconds before the universe struck again in
Interesting Times.)

12 . . . he is tired of ankle-deep slurry.* (*Mort*)

---

* Dr Johnson said something similar about London. But not very.

Faculty of
PSEUDONYMY II

Give an alternative name for each of the
following . . .

1 'Charcoal.'

2 Pongo.

3 Lias Bluestone.

4 Henry Slugg.

5 Mr Stuffed Tube.

6 Known to dwarfs as *K'ez'rek
d'b'duz* ('Go Around the Other
Side of the Mountain').

7 Edward d'Eath.

8 The Supreme Grand Master.

9 Tempscire.

10 Delores de Syn.

Faculty of Pseudonymy II
ANSWERS

1 The Ephebian philosopher Abraxas, who interviewed several gods while researching his agnostic tract *On Religion* and was duly struck by lightning at least 15 times. Remembered for his aphorism that gods like to see an atheist around; it gives them something to aim at. (*Small Gods*)

2 The Librarian, so-called to allow him to travel free as a pet on the coach to Lancre. Taxonomists have a nasty habit of calling the orang-utan *Pongo pygmaeus*, meaning a small Pongo. (*Lords and Ladies*)

3 Cliff – the troll drummer's *nom de* Music With Rocks In. (*Soul Music*)

4 Señor Enrico Basilica, opera tenor whose fame was even huger than his body. Just. (*Maskerade*)

5 Ronald 'Teach' Saveloy – a literal Agatean translation of his surname. (*Interesting Times*)

6 Granny Weatherwax again . . . (*Maskerade*)

7 Beano the Clown – a sinister impersonation carried out by the Assassin and monarchist d'Eath as part of his doomed plot. (*Men at Arms*)

8 Lupine Wonse. (*Guards! Guards!*)

9 A literal French translation of Weatherwax, used as an impenetrable alias by Granny's sister Lilith/Lily. (*Witches Abroad*)

10 Theda 'Ginger' Withel's screen-name when starring in various Sargers of Passione in a Worlde Gonne Madde. (*Moving Pictures*)

Faculty of ELDRITCH SYNCHRONICITY II

Once again, who or what from outside Discworld was, or could plausibly be argued to be, the original of or at least a distant inspiration for . . .

1 Bravd and the Weasel?

2 Bloody Stupid Johnson?

3 The mystic Ching Aling of the Hublandish folk?

4 The Old Kingdom of Djelibeybi?

5 Brutha, novice of the Omnian church?

6 Creosote's bijou wildernessette?

7 Fliemoe the bully?

8 The god Hoki?

9 The near-tragic accident from which Nanny Ogg is saved only by the special willow-reinforced hat made for her by Mr Vernissage of Slice?

10 The Assassins' Guild practical examination?

Faculty of Eldritch Synchronicity II
ANSWERS

1   These freebooters from *The Colour of Magic* seem
    distantly reminiscent of Fritz Leiber's characters Fafhrd
    and the Grey Mouser.

2   Not a dig at the late British novelist B.S. Johnson. The
    name of Discworld's most fabulously inept architect
    and landscape gardener echoes England's 18th-
    century master of garden design, Capability Brown
    (real forename Lancelot) – who gets a direct mention in
    Men at Arms, along with the less plausible Sagacity
    Smith and Intuition De Vere Slade-Gore . . .

3   The inscrutable Chinese *I Ching* system of divination –
    only on Discworld the patterns are octograms rather
    than the *I Ching*'s hexagrams. (*Mort*)

4   Ancient Egypt.* (*Pyramids*)

5   Brutha's build, his powerful mind, and the fact that his
    fellow-novices call him the Big Dumb Ox, should
    remind the discerning of St Thomas Aquinas. (*Small
    Gods*)

---

* Known to Egyptologists as the Old Kingdom. This is why they find
such side-splitting hilarity in graffiti like KHUFU RULES OK.

6   It is a gentle running gag that this walled garden has been landscaped in accordance with at least some of Coleridge's description of Xanadu in 'Kubla Khan'. (*Sourcery*)

7   Part of the Assassins' School episode in *Pyramids* pays homage to *Tom Brown's Schooldays* (1857) by Thomas Hughes, with Fliemoe taking the approximate rôle of the bully Flashman.* The warning, 'If he invites you for toast in his study, *don't go*', should remind Hughes fans of the Flashman gang's favourite torture.

8   Pan, like Hoki, is your standard nature god who tends to manifest as half-man, half-goat, and play the flute – in Hoki's case, very badly. (*Equal Rites*) There's a touch of another mischievous god there, too, in the name and the fact that Hoki got chucked out of Dunmanifestin (Abode of the Gods) for pulling the old exploding mistletoe joke on Blind Io . . . so half a mark if you said Loki.

9   The farmhouse that lands on Nanny's head in *Witches Abroad* is, of course, a graceful homage to the one which a cyclone blows from Kansas to Oz in L. Frank Baum's *The Wizard of Oz* (1900), fortuitously killing the Wicked Witch of the East when it lands. As Nanny resonantly remarks to her cat: 'You know, Greebo, I don't think we're in Lancre.' Besides the book there is the film, noted in *Moving Pictures* as being about a yellow sick toad . . .

10 Suspiciously reminiscent of a British driving test. Especially the bit where the sadistic examiner asks his victim to identify a sign held upside-down. (*Pyramids*)

This is how the Pratchett mind works: Flashman in *Tom Brown's Schooldays* has a crony called Speedicut, which is or was a make of lawnmower, as of course is Flymo, and . . .

Faculty of
COLOPHONICS

. . . or *Famous Last Words*. Which characters signed off with these majestically memorable phrases?

1 Thought so.

2 I'll think about it.

3 Yes. There is that.

4 Yes. Yes, of course.

5 But I don't *believe* in reincarnation!

6 Let *everyone* see what happens.

7 I wouldn't like to think I'd suffered much . . . What happens now?

8 On the whole, I think it's worth a try.

9 More than 1300, I'm afraid.

10 Are there going to be . . . choirs and things?

11 But the song says it's the terrible desert –

12 I *like* it.

Bonus question: Which of these remarks is unusual in its timing?

Faculty of Colophonics
ANSWERS

1 Deccan Ribobe. (*Moving Pictures*)

2 Bjorn Hammerhock in *Men at Arms*, puzzling over Death's chummy suggestion that, with reincarnation, he could soon be Bjorn again.

3 Drum Billet. (*Equal Rites*)

4 Vorbis. (*Small Gods*)

5 Mr Pounder, in the process of being reincarnated as a rat. (*Maskerade*)

6 Lord Hong. (*Interesting Times*)

7 Zebbo Mooty, Thief Third Class. (*Guards! Guards!*)

8 Mr Saveloy in *Interesting Times*, delighted to get a chance of Valhalla instead of wherever schoolteachers normally go. (He had a horrible suspicion that it would be full of sports masters.)

9 The massed mummies of Djelibeybi. (*Pyramids*)

10 Dr Undershaft the chorus master. (*Maskerade*)

11 General Fri'it of Omnia. (*Small Gods*)

12 Beano the Clown in *Men at Arms*, on hearing from Death that the afterlife – whatever mysteries it may contain – does *not* feature custard pies, red noses, juggling or baggy trousers.

Bonus mark: Lord Hong was the only one of those above to utter the cited last words before actually dying.

Faculty of
EGREGIOSITY IV

Spot the one in each set that sticks out like
something notoriously famed for sticking out . . .

1 Quezovercoatl, Urglefloggah, Astfgl, Rerpf, WxrtHltl-
   jwlpklz, Riinjswin.

2 Spime, Wasp Agaric, Achorion Purple, Mustick.

3 Chondrodite, Carbonaceous, Gigalith, Silicarous,
   Monolith.

4 Chiming sundial, Quirm Memorial, Hanging Gardens of
   Ankh, Triumphal Arch, Brass Bridge, Colossus of
   Morpork.

5 Count, Duke, Squire, Earl, King.

6 Untied Alchemists, Microlithic Pictures, Century of the
   Fruitbat, ParaMountain, Fir Wood Studios.

7 *Bumper Fun Book, Bumper Fun Grimoire, Monster Fun
   Book, Monster Fun Grimoire.*

8 Voltan the Indestructible, The Immortal Jenkins, Hrun the
   Barbarian, Crowdie the Strong, Organdy Sloggo, Slasher
   Mungo, Gosbar the Wake.

9 Varnishes, Glazes, Creams, Zuumchats, Zoons, Punes.

10 Juf, Ket, Ptah, Put, Scrab, Teppicymon XXVII, Thrrp,
   Vut.

ANSWERS

1 All are demons except Rerpf, an Ankh-Morpork merchant.

2 The last three are poisons suitable for administration by ear. Spime, contrariwise, is a snake-venom antidote obtained from the liver of the inflatable mongoose. (*Pyramids*)

3 All are troll gods except Carbonaceous, an ordinary troll. (*Moving Pictures*)

4 All are creations of the architect, landscape designer and organ bodger Bloody Stupid Johnson – except the Brass Bridge. (*Men at Arms*, *Interesting Times*)

5 Except for Count, these are the names of the Bottomley brothers – whose parents had upwardly mobile but slightly simplistic notions about class structure. (*Reaper Man*)

6 All are click-making outfits except ParaMountain – Holy Wood Hill itself is the ParaMountain, according to that mystic chronicle of yore *The Boke of the Film*. (*Moving Pictures*)

7 All are authentic Discworld tomes except (at least so far) the *Bumper Fun Book*.

8 All are former barbarian heroes who, to the dismay of Cohen, prove to be dead – with the exception of Hrun, whom a worse fate befell. He got a job. With a pension. (*Interesting Times*)

9 All are things whose making have been taught to Esk (or so she claims) by Granny Weatherwax . . . except Zoons, who are the people she is boasting to.* (*Equal Rites*)

10 All are gods of Djelibeybi except Ptah, a god of our own world's Ancient Egypt. (*Pyramids*)

* It is not known whether punes are related to that popular Discworld figure of speech the pune, or play on words.

Faculty of
SPELLAEOLOGY

From the eldritch armouries of wizardry, what spells or devices would you choose to obtain the following effects?

1 Escaping the cares of the world to have a quiet smoke.

2 Transforming foes into worms.

3 A nice bunch of flowers in an emergency.

4 Converting a bandit chief to a pumpkin.

5 Manoeuvring an extremely heavy and obstreperous burden over a high wall.

6 Causing your foe to fall sideways to the wall and stick there.

7 A violent, localized earthquake.

8 The creation, evolution, flourishing and extinction of a race of giant reptiles, all in about five minutes.

9 Enumerating clergymen.

10 The proper hatching of turtle eggs.

Faculty of Spellaeology
ANSWERS

1 Maligree's Wonderful Garden. (*Sourcery*)

2 Turning to Animals – an Eighth Level spell. (*The Colour of Magic*)

3 Eringyas' Surprising Bouquet. (*Reaper Man*)

4 Stacklady's Morphic Resonator. (*Lords and Ladies*)

5 Gindle's Effortless Elevator. (*Moving Pictures*)

6 Atavarr's Personal Gravitational Upset. (*The Colour of Magic*)

7 Herpetty's Seismic Reorganizer. (*Reaper Man*)

8 Pelepel's Temporal Compressor. (*Sourcery*)

9 'Numbers' Riktor's Rev Counter for Use in Ecclesiastical Areas. (*Moving Pictures*)

10 All eight nameless spells from that primal grimoire the Octavo. (*The Light Fantastic*)

Faculty of
'OOK II

Further neatly shelved questions about oookish matters . . .

1 Where is the biggest non-magical library in the world?

2 What was Translated from the Khalian by A Gentleman, with Hand-Coloured Plates for the Connoisseur in A Strictly Limited Edition?

3 What seems so curiously self-referential about Humptulip's epic 2000-page work of nonfiction?

4 What delicate surgical operation was carried out by the Librarian?

5 What begins with 'Lesson One: Fairy Footsteps'?

6 Which dread book gave rise to a whole textbook in which it is Discussed for Students, With Practical Experiments?

7 Which book begins with an Author's Note ending NOW READ ON?

8 Who wrote *Along the Ankh with Bow, Rod, and Staff with a Knob on the End*?

9 What was the crude volume that listed only women's names and sums of money?

10 Which celebrated work of philosophy contains the maxim, 'It's a rum old world all right. But you've got to laugh, haven't you?'

Faculty of Oook II
ANSWERS

1 For a long while it was in Ephebe, but by the end of *Small Gods* it is in the Citadel of Kom, chief city of Omnia. A mark for either answer; a bonus mark if you got both.

2 *The Shuttered Palace*, a confusing but instructive work of erotic reference which leaves young readers well prepared for chaps who try to introduce them to certain athletic techniques favoured by the classical Pseudopolitans. (*Pyramids*)

3 Its title is *How to Kille Insects . . .* (*Men at Arms*)

4 An appendectomy on a book damaged in the rush when the Library took flight. (*Sourcery*)

5 *Blert Wheedown's Guitar Primer*. 'Play your Way to Succefs in Three Easy Lefsons and Eighteen Hard Lefsons'. (*Soul Music*)

6 The *Necrotelecomnicon*. Giving students a sanitized textbook rather than the grimoire itself prevented various problems such as insanity, brains dribbling out of ears, flesh crawling off hands and up arms, etc. (*Moving Pictures*)

7 *Lords and Ladies* by Terry Pratchett. It is not known whether Unseen University Library has a copy – but the Librarian will know where to find it, through L-space if necessary.

8 Mustrum Ridcully, Archchancellor of Unseen University. (*Soul Music*)

9 Captain Vimes's record of his furtive hand-outs to the widows and orphans of deceased Guard members. (*Men at Arms*)

10 Didactylos's *Meditations*. (*Small Gods*)

Faculty of
LINGUISTICS II

Another clutch of non-Common Tongue
expressions for you to interpret. Can you do as
well as Nanny Ogg?

1   Archaic Ankh-Morporkian: *Sodomy non sapiens.*

2   Assassins' jargon: Priests.

3   Trob or beTrobi: *[censored . . . the worst word in the
    language].*

4   Tree marking: *dot dot dot dash dot dash.*

5   Magical-taxonomic: *tabernae vagantes.*

6   K'turni: *p'ch'zarni'chiwkov.*

7   Medical jargon: *mortis portalis tackulatum.*

8   Rhyming slang: Ronald.

9   Cumhoolie: *squernt.*

10 Psychological jargon: *reja vu.*

ANSWERS

1 'I'm buggered if I know.' Not all readers twigged that when Albert says this in *Mort* he is not expressing ignorance but giving the translation.

2 Protective overshoes for coping with poisoned spikes and caltraps, so-called because they save your soles. (*Pyramids*)

3 'Such a one who, while wearing a copper nose-ring, stands in a footbath atop Mount Raruaruaha during a heavy thunderstorm and shouts that Alohura, Goddess of Lightning, has the facial features of a diseased uloruaha root!' (*The Colour of Magic*)

4 Your location is 'Hub-by-Turnwise, one mile from the village' ... of Bad Ass. (*Equal Rites*)

5 'Wandering shops' – those magically appearing shops that sell you strange and wondrous things but usually aren't there when you go back to complain they don't work. (*The Light Fantastic*)

6 'The nasty little sound of a sword being unsheathed right behind one at just the point when one thought one had disposed of one's enemies.' (*Equal Rites*)

7 'Dead as a doornail.' (*Pyramids*)

8 Apparently 'turd' – the unpleasant Ronald the Third of Lancre being remembered by this rhyme alone.* (*Witches Abroad*)

9 'The feeling upon finding that the previous occupant of the privy has used all the paper.' (*Equal Rites*).

10 Opposite of *déjà vu* ... 'I am going to be here again.' (*Pyramids*)

---

* In Britain, owing to the bad press he got from the Tudors and Shakespeare, the word is 'Richard'.

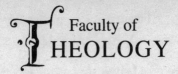

Faculty of THEOLOGY

Questions relating to the Discworld's awesome
spiritual beings and religious orders . . .

1   Who was Hat?

2   What single word means 'A short and unnecessary
    religious observance performed daily by the Holy
    Balancing Dervishes of Otherz'?

3   Whose was the five-metre mountain troll that found itself
    teleported to confront Rincewind and Twoflower?

4   Highly skilled Listening Monks can hear frozen echoes in
    ammonites and amber. What substance did the best of
    them all listen to?

5   Which god is about three feet high with floppy rabbit
    ears, tiny horns and an extremely good turn of speed,
    normally used to the full?

6   Who uses a variety of false noses and 70 different
    hammers to be the thunder god of *every* Discworld
    pantheon?

7   Whose sacred symbol was a matched set of flying ducks?

8   What symbolic object represents Patina, Ephebian
    Goddess of Wisdom?

9   There were eight of them, led by – to the best of anyone's
    recollection – Cantaloupe. Who were they?

10 Which god's priest felt impelled to shout an impassioned
    sports commentary into a bulrush, and was then thrown to
    the crocodiles?

11 Who is an appropriately named god of the winds?

12 Could this be the god of supermarkets?

Faculty of Theology

ANSWERS

1 The Vulture-Headed God of Unexpected Guests. (*Pyramids*)

2 Tridlins – according to the *Dictionary of Eye-Watering Words*. (*Guards! Guards!*)

3 A gameboard piece of Offler the Crocodile God. The fact that it is instantly killed by way of a mind-wrenching coincidence could not, of course, possibly have anything to do with Lady Luck's stake in the same game. (*The Colour of Magic*)

4 Basalt. The others heard the sound before the noise at the Beginning: 'One, Two, Three, Four.' He detected the sound before that: 'One, Two . . .' (*Soul Music*)

5 Herne the Hunted, god of small doomed furry creatures everywhere. Let us prey. (*Wyrd Sisters*, *Lords and Ladies*)

6 Blind Io . . . at least according to Om, who as a god himself should know. (*Small Gods*)

7 Ordpor the Tasteless. (*Reaper Man*)

8 A penguin. The sculptor, it is hinted, may have intended some other bird, and here we remember that Pallas Athene went around with an owl . . . (*Small Gods*)

9 The Muses of Discworld, believed by the Ephebians to inspire musicians and artists. Cantaloupe ('I'm pretty sure it wasn't Cantaloupe') is a dim echo of Calliope, head girl of Greek mythology's nine Muses. (*Soul Music*)

10 Cephut, the Old Kingdom's God of Cutlery. (*Pyramids*)

11 Flatulus, from the large Ephebian pantheon. (*Small Gods*)

12 Mister Safe Way, one of the voodoo gods invented by Mrs Erzulie* Gogol in *Witches Abroad*, echoes the Safeway supermarket chain. This, says Terry Pratchett, was inspired by a local chain he came across, called Carrefour . . . irresistibly reminding him of Maître Carrefour, Lord of the Crossroads, from the 'real' voodoo pantheon.

---

* Of course *you* knew that Erzulie is the name of another voodoo *loa* or spirit . . .

Faculty of 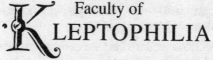KLEPTOPHILIA

What was stolen . . .

1 From the library of Unseen University?

2 From the altar of the Temple of Offler, by Brother Charnel?

3 From within the Troll's Head, by Larry the Fox alias Fezzy the Stoat?

4 From the gods, by Fingers-Mazda?

5 From the Archmage of Ymitury?

6 From the Opera House, subsequently seen making away on at least seven legs of various sizes?

7 From the *Odium*?

8 From the Lost Jewelled Temple of Doom of Offler the Crocodile God in darkest Howondaland?

9 From Unseen University, and subsequently taken to Klatch?

10 From the Assassins' Guild museum?

11 From the impregnable palace of the Archmandrite of B'Tuni?

12 Temporarily, from the vicinity of Sator Square, as a student prank?

ANSWERS

1 Tubal de Malachite's *The Summoning of Dragons*, taken by Brother Fingers. (*Guards! Guards!*)

2 The altar gold, which he made into a horn that played magical music – immortalizing him in musical history as Felonious Monk. (*Soul Music*)

3 The Archchancellor's Hat – a course of action which proved unwise. (*Sourcery*)

4 Fire. But he couldn't fence it because it was too hot. (*Men at Arms*)

5 His staff, his belt of moon jewels, and his life, in approximately that order – by the Weasel, or so he claimed. (*The Colour of Magic*)

6 A piano. (*Soul Music*)

7 Some significant footage of rocks from the click *Shadowe of the Dessert*, bitten out by the Librarian. (*Moving Pictures*)

8 The Tear of Offler, largest diamond in the world, removed from the great jewel-encrusted statue of Offler Himself by Death. (*Reaper Man*) According to Twoflower in *The Light Fantastic*, Cohen the Barbarian also once stole the sacred diamond from the giant statue of Offler. Perhaps it was replaced. Perhaps it was a different giant statue. Who knows?

9 The Archchancellor's Hat, by Conina. (*Sourcery*)

10 The 'gonne' devised by Leonard of Quirm. (*Men at Arms*)

11 The sword Kring, by Hrun the Barbarian. (*The Colour of Magic*)

12 Unseen University. (*Soul Music*)

Faculty of
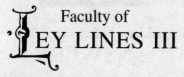EY LINES III

Yet again, what's the Discworld connection (or plausible morphic resonance) of . . .

1 Cleopatra?

2 Ernst Stavro Blofeld?

3 Federal Express?

4 J.R. 'Bob' Dobbs, High Epopt of the Church of the SubGenius?

5 Beowulf?

6 Light-bulb jokes?

7 AREPO TENET OPERA ROTAS?

8 Jack Vance?

9 *A Dictionary of Historical Slang* by Eric Partridge?

10 Trivial Pursuit?

Faculty of Ley Lines III
ANSWERS

1   Apparently Queen Ezeriel of Klatch, who had a lot of lovers, took baths in asses' milk and tragically sat on an asp. (*Mort*)

2   This James Bond movie villain's habit of delicately caressing a white cat while sentencing people to horrible deaths is mentioned, in *Sourcery*, as being very much in the manner of the Patrician.

3   The Ephebian messenger of the gods is called not Mercury but, we regret to remind you, Fedecks. (*Small Gods*)

4   Strange but true: the graphic novel of *The Light Fantastic* (part II, page 6) inserts a picture of 'Bob' into the Discworld zodiac as 'Okjock the Salesman'. There may even be a reason for this.

5   A parody of the Beowulf legend appears just for fun in *Guards! Guards!* as an example of how uppity monsters are getting these days: '. . . This guy, he killed this monster . . . no problem, stuck its arm up over the door . . . and you know what? Its mum come and complained. Its actual mum come right down to the hall next day and *complained*.'

6   On Discworld, of course, they tell lamp-wick jokes: 'How many trolls . . . ?' (*Sourcery*)

7 Four lines of an ancient and celebrated palindromic 5x5 word-square, sometimes known (from the here-omitted first line) as the Sator Square. Of course Sator Square is a well-known feature of Ankh-Morpork city. *Pedant alert:* this Latin word-square is sometimes called early-Christian, but may date back to 79 BC or earlier since it was found on a plaster column at Pompeii.

8 A bit remote, we admit, but Jack Vance's ideas of magic in *The Dying Earth* (1950) established the fantasy tradition of spells being named after their creators ('Phandaal's Mantle of Stealth'), being difficult to force into your head, occupying valuable mental space while there, and getting 'used up' when spoken. This spread widely via the Dungeons & Dragons game (which, ahem, paid extensive homage to Vance's system), and was thus a natural for adoption and gentle parody in Discworld.

9 Versions of long-ago catch-phrases listed in this and other references are woven into Discworld dialogue. Thus the wizard Windle Poons – as befits his great age – comes up with such 19th-century expressions of derision as 'Draw it mild!', 'How's your granny off for soap?' and 'Twopence more and up goes the donkey!' (*Moving Pictures*)

10 The Discworld gods play, instead, Significant Quest. (*Sourcery*)

Faculty of
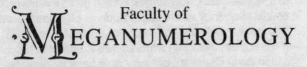
MEGANUMEROLOGY

All the answers here are numbers of three or more
digits. There are built-in hints.

1 What is the result of dividing the height plus length of the
Great Pyramid of Tsort by half its width? (Apart from the
expected slight headache, that is.)

Alternative and slightly easier question: What is the number
on Captain Vimes's Ankh-Morpork City Guard (Night
Watch) badge?

2 Roughly how long ago was Unseen University founded?

3 How many approved jokes are allowed to members of the
Guild of Fools and Joculators?

4 Which Abbot of the History Monks sent Lu-Tze on his
mission and later played chess with Death?

5 How many Commandments were written on the Citadel
door in Kom?

6 Where in nightmarish Elm Street did the Fresh Start Club
meet?

7 Roughly how old is the Old Kingdom of Djelibeybi?

8 What is the number of the octogram which in a certain
divination system is called Illegality, the Unatoning
Goose?

9 In which year did King Gruneberry the Good of Lancre
die?

10 *How* many elephants?

ANSWERS

The incredibly subtle numbering of the questions was meant to help you recall these big numbers . . . Indeed, if you worked this out and could thus be confident about the first digit in each case, give yourself half a mark per answer even if you didn't know any of the rest of the number.

1   1.67563, or 1,237.98712567 times the difference between the distance to the sun and the weight of a small orange. A mark for any figure within 20 per cent, or for just remembering the bit about the sun and the orange. (*The Light Fantastic*) If you opted for the alternative question: Vimes's badge number was 177. (*Men at Arms*)

2   Approximately 2000 years. (*Mort*)

3   383 are recorded in the Guild's solemn *Monster Fun Book*. Official new jokes may with great difficulty be added – the grandfather of the Fool in *Wyrd Sisters* was responsible for seven, but then he was a four-time consecutive winner of the Grand Prix des Idiots Blithering.

4   The 493rd. His name is not recorded. (*Small Gods*)

5   512, with more expected when the Eighth Prophet of Om made his appearance.* It makes you realize how virtually irreligious it must be to get by with just ten commandments. (*Small Gods*)

6   668 (*Reaper Man*) This reminds us that a planned but never written sequel to the Gaiman/Pratchett *Good Omens* was to have been called *668: The Neighbour of the Beast*.

7   Some 7000 years. (*Pyramids*)

8   8887. (*Mort*)

9   967. (*Wyrd Sisters*)

10 'With a 1000 Elephants!' (*Moving Pictures*)

* Although things worked out rather differently in the end.

Faculty of
GASTROLOGY III

Surely just one more nibble at this theme wouldn't
affect the day's calorie count . . .

1 According to the recipe they start out as Maids of
   Honour, but . . .

2 It's advisable, indeed essential, to remove every bit of its
   stomach, liver and digestive tract before eating.

3 This was vaguely round, of a woodish texture, and when
   struck made a noise like a ruler plucked over the edge of
   a desk.

4 It was green and had to be repeatedly hit with a spoon to
   stop it getting away.

5 The difference between Lancre and Quirm cheese.

6 The Bursar of Unseen University thought this particular
   outlay was 'tremendous value for money'.

7 From an underdog's viewpoint, this is the special
   attraction of the Assassins' Guild on Wednesday nights.

8 The socio-political equivalent, on the Counterweight
   Continent, of apple pie in the United States.

9 For proper savour it should be dropped in rivers and dried
   out and sat on and left and looked at every day and put
   away again.

10 Its lack of mayonnaise adversely affected the entire
    course of Discworld life.

Faculty of Gastrology III
ANSWERS

1 '. . . they ends up Tarts.' This is all too characteristic of Nanny Ogg's gourmet treats. (*Maskerade*)

2 Perhaps the most expensive item on a *squishi* menu: deep sea blowfish, *Singularis minutia gigantica*, whose organs are the source of the poison 'bloat'. Eat an improperly prepared portion and every cell in your body instantly tries to swell to 2000 times its former size. They don't need to bury you, just redecorate over the top. (*Pyramids*)

3 Dwarf cake. 'One tiny piece of this and you won't want anything to eat all day.' (*Guards! Guards!*) Half a mark for naming, instead, the similarly but not quite identically described dwarf *bread* found elsewhere . . .

4 Yoghurt – *live* yoghurt – a bargain offer from Cut-Me-Own-Hand-Off Dhblah. 'Onna stick!' (*Small Gods*)

5 Lancre cheese is the one with the holes; Quirm cheese is the one with the blue veins. (*Soul Music*)

6 The salary of 'the best Librarian we've ever had' – which is, naturally, peanuts. (*Moving Pictures*)

7 The cook does a mixed grill and no one ever eats the black pudding – a golden begging opportunity for Gaspode the Wonder Dog. (*Men at Arms*)

8 Raw fish. American ideals (as expressed in feelgood political speeches) are traditionally supposed to include motherhood and apple pie; in *Interesting Times*, Two Little Wang has similar feelings about 'motherhood and raw fish'.

9 Dwarf bread. It's even better if the cat's pissed on it. (*Witches Abroad*)

10 The not very nice egg-and-cress sandwich given to Rincewind by the Creator Himself in the void shortly before the Beginning: 'Let there be egg and cress, sort of thing.' Life subsequently evolved from its wisely unfinished remains. (*Eric*)

Faculty of HEADOLOGY

A quick test of wits. Which witch . . .

1 Bequeathed the pumpkin-fixated wand?

2 Created quite an easy recipe for filling people's bones with hot lead ('What you do is, you get some lead . . .')?

3 Made Destiny an offer it couldn't refuse?

4 Was helpfully instrumental in preventing any overcrowding in the town of Ohulan Cutash?

5 Suffered a temporary haunting of her apron?

6 Was envied by Granny Weatherwax for having lost all her teeth by age 20 and gained real crone-credibility?

7 Went out Borrowing one day, never came back, and is suspected of now being a local bluetit?

8 Was temporally unfocused owing to a detached retina in her second sight?

9 Taught witchcraft to Granny Weatherwax?

10 Was briefly known as Fairy Hedgehog?

11 Had a front elevation resembling an ironing board with a couple of peas on it?

12 Is obscurely reminiscent of the novels *Dead Souls* (1842) and *King Solomon's Mines* (1885)?

ANSWERS

1 Desiderata Hollow. (*Witches Abroad*)

2 Goodie Whemper, she who trained Magrat Garlick as a witch and must share the blame. (*Wyrd Sisters*)

3 Lily Weatherwax, the Godmother. (*Witches Abroad*)

4 Hilta Goatfounder, vendor of Madame Goatfounder's Pennyroyal Preventives. (*Equal Rites*)

5 Nanny Ogg. The haunter – 'Not the first, either' – was King Verence I. (*Wyrd Sisters*)

6 Nanny Annapple. (*Equal Rites*)

7 Granny Postalute. For years Nanny Ogg put out lumps of fat and bacon rind for the bluetit, just in case. (*Lords and Ladies*)

8 Old Mother Dismass. (*Witches Abroad*)

9 Nanny Gripes.* As Granny boasted, this 'took her a week *and* I had the afternoons free'. (*Lords and Ladies*)

10 Nanny Ogg, thanks to her regrettable habit of singing 'The Hedgehog Song' on all inappropriate occasions.** (*Witches Abroad*)

11 Magrat Garlick. (*Wyrd Sisters*)

12 Mrs Gogol of Genua in *Witches Abroad*. *Dead Souls* is by the noted Russian author Nikolai Gogol; *King Solomon's Mines* by H. Rider Haggard features a very much nastier black witch called Gagool.

---

* If you named Goodie Filter . . . good try, but *Wyrd Sisters* merely indicates that Goodie Filter was a sharp-spoken senior witch in the coven which had Esme Weatherwax in the youngest, or Magrat, rôle.

** Thaumaturgical research has yet to discover an appropriate one.

Faculty of
QUAFFICULTURE

Yet again, the items indicated are all of a kind.

1 The first thing (or first eight things) that Henry Slugg wanted after announcing that he'd chewed his last tentacle.

2 Rincewind had the idea that houris were little tubes used to suck it up.

3 Manufactured from cactus sap and scorpion venom.

4 It should never be allowed to come into contact with metal.

5 Nanny Ogg's special distilled version of the foregoing.

6 Gives you a bad time several hours before the event.

7 Found by cutting open the fleshy leaves of stone plants.

8 Normal contents of a certain bottom drawer in the Watch House.

9 A silvery, desiccated residue easily reconstituted by adding water.

10 The known preference of Pestilence.

ANSWERS

Cheers! Or as they put it in *Wellcome to Ankh-Morporke, Citie of One Thousand Surprises*, '. . . raise your Glass convivial and say: "Cheer! Here looking, you Kid! Up, You Bottom!"'

1 Eight pints of Turbot's Really Odd. (*Maskerade*)

2 Sherbet. (*The Light Fantastic*)

3 Orakh, a virulently alcoholic Klatchian beverage. (*Sourcery*)

4 Scumble. (*Mort*)

5 Suicider. (*Maskerade*)

6 *Vul* nut wine, or any other Discworld drink made from reannual fruit so that you get the hangover first. (*The Colour of Magic*)

7 Up to half a pint of water which unfortunately 'tastes like weewee'. (*Small Gods*)

8 Jimkin Bearhugger's Old Selected Dragon's Blood Whiskey,* the favourite reality-repellant of Captain Vimes. (*Guards! Guards!*) Later, however, having married his Sybil, he gave up alcohol entirely, and even went along to meetings and things.

9 Dehydrated water, which is found at the heart of the Great Nef desert and supports some very strange fish. (*The Colour of Magic*)

10 A small egg nog with a cherry in it. (*Sourcery*)

---

* Also useful for cleaning spoons.

Faculty of
ANCILLARY PERSONAGES II

Concerning another batch of Discworld's minor characters, spear-carriers and walk-ons . . .

1 Old Shaker Wistley from Creel Springs in the Ramtops was a bit of a fetishist who had to go for a lie-down if he became over-excited by the sight of a woman (even Nanny Ogg) wearing . . . what?

2 Which frightfully respectable female institution was run by Miss Eulalie Butts?

3 How did Drumknott, clerk to the Patrician, help fuel a message-carrying Pointless Albatross for its return journey to the Agatean Empire?

4 Reg Plenty fell into the curdling vats during a possible quarrel and became part of the finest Farmhouse Nutty that Mr Bucket's firm had ever made. But what was the drawback?

5 Second cousin !Kck! had responsibility for the whole of the Green Section of which vast herd?

6 What was the family business of Ptaclusp, father of one born architect and cosmic engineer, and one born accountant?

7 For what surface quality was Pewsey Ogg, son of Jason and grandson of Nanny, best known?

8 What was the aim of Lord Vassenego's utterly diabolical plan against Astfgl, King of Hell?

9 Ovin Hakardly, a Seventh Level wizard who had somehow developed the ability to pronounce punctuation, had an abstract concern for Lore which gave him the courage or sheer stark idiocy to tick off the most dangerous person on Discworld at that time. Who was the person?

10 Who was the psychopathic poodle leader of Ankh-Morpork's least-known guild?

ANSWERS

1 Boots. Especially black buttoned boots. His tastes were a bit *sophisticated*. (*Witches Abroad*)

2 She was the conscientious headmistress of the Quirm College for Young Ladies. (*Soul Music*)

3 He usefully found a bottle of fishpaste in the Palace kitchens. (*Interesting Times*)

4 The presence of Reg Plenty's trouser buttons in the cheese used to be one of Mr Bucket's biggest worries.* (*Maskerade*)

5 The 1000 elephants whose epic delivery from Howondaland to Ankh-Morpork was organized by skilled kilopachydermatolist M'Bu. (*Moving Pictures*)

6 Constructing pyramids and related items: the business was Ptaclusp Associates, Necropolitan Builders to the Dynasties. (*Pyramids*)

7 Pewsey was generally recognized as the stickiest known child in the multiverse. (*Lords and Ladies*)

8 To kick him upstairs, or downstairs: Vassenego finally persuaded Astfgl to accept the token position of Supreme Life President of Hell. With executive toys. (*Eric*)

9 Coin, the Sourcerer. (*Sourcery*)

10 Big Fido, berserk poodle founder and leader of the Dogs' Guild. (*Men at Arms*)

* Another being when young Weevins minced his thumb in the stirring machine. It was sheer luck that they happened to be making strawberry yoghurt at the time.

Faculty of PROBABILITY ANALYSIS

Spot the thing or event or context being referred to:

1 IT WOULD BE A MILLION TO ONE CHANCE. EXACTLY A MILLION TO ONE CHANCE.

2 Scientists have calculated that the chance of anything so patently absurd existing are millions to one.

3 'Million to one chance. It'd escaped from a menagerie . . .'

4 'Five hundred and thirty-eight to one. I calculated that.'

5 It was a million-to-one chance, with any luck.

6 'It's a 999,943-to-one chance but it might just work.'

7 I DON'T KNOW. IT'S A MILLION TO ONE CHANCE.

8 They said you had one chance in two unless you drew old Mericet . . .

9 '. . . everything has to happen somewhere, d'ye see, so that means it *could* happen here. Even if it's a million to one chance, ma'am.'

10 '"It's a million to one chance,"' said Lady Ramkin, 'I think he said, "but it might just work."'

11 'It's a million-to-one chance,' he [Rincewind] said, 'but it might just work . . .'

12 'Million-to-one chances,' she [Granny Weatherwax] said, 'crop up nine times out of ten.'

Faculty of Probability Analysis
ANSWERS

1 Rincewind's return home from the Dungeon Dimensions. (*Eric*)

2 The Discworld itself. (*Mort*)

3 Being bitten by a crocodile in the streets of Ankh-Morpork. (*Guards! Guards!*)

4 According to Twoflower, the odds against a house catching fire in the Red Triangle district of Bes Pelargic. (*The Colour of Magic*)

5 Om, in his tortoise incarnation, getting to the Citadel in time via eagle-lift. (*Small Gods*)

6 Something, according to Carrot, which no one would ever say. It's million-to-one or nothing. (*Guards! Guards!*)

7 That Death's plan to fight the New Death with the ghost of his superlatively sharpened scythe-blade will work. (*Reaper Man*)

8 Passing the Assassins' examination. (*Pyramids*)

9 That Lancre's pitifully small forces could defeat the fearsome elves – argued by Ridcully from his wobbly understanding of the many-worlds quantum theory. (*Lords and Ladies*)

10 A successful relationship between Captain Vimes and Lady Ramkin – Sergeant Colon's estimate of the odds. (*Guards! Guards!*)

11 The plan to panic the Agatean forces with rumours about 2,300,009 invisible vampire ghosts.* (*Interesting Times*)

12 Recovering Esk's staff, which she threw into the now rapidly flooding River Ankh. (*Equal Rites*)

---

* Just *possibly* a sly allusion to the similar stratagem in Eric Frank Russell's sf novel *Next of Kin* (1958), alias *The Space Willies*.

Faculty of
ADHESIVE
ULTIMATES II

A further selection of sticky ends ... suffered by whom?

1   Flash-frozen and shattered.

2   Drank a rejuvenating draught from the Fountain of Youth (which is in Forn Parts) and neglected to boil it first.

3   Went mountain climbing at the age of 119. Last recorded words: 'Oh bugger.'

4   The result of personally testing whether a broomstick could, in fact, survive having its bristles pulled out one by one in mid-air.

5   Temporarily believing oneself to be a seagull while at the top of a 100ft wall.

6   Stabbed-through by a unicorn's horn while hunting out of season.

7   Being shot for the sake of the Truth and to save a revered philosopher.

8   Lighting a pipe after half a pint of Wow-Wow Sauce (which contains sulphur and saltpetre for added potency) followed by a charcoal biscuit to settle his stomach.

9   Begging for an ending and being rewarded by a woodcutter's axe.

10 Reduced to a small heap of charcoal while partway through uttering a rude word – the first person to die in such a fashion for centuries.

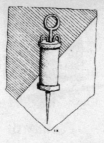

Faculty of Adhesive Ultimates II
ANSWERS

1 The thief Larry the Fox or Fezzy the Stoat. (*Sourcery*)

2 Ponce da Quirm. (*Eric*)

3 The witch Gammer (Old Mabel) Peavey. It was the way she would have wanted to go. (*Witches Abroad*)

4 The witch Goodie Whemper. The answer to the question she was researching was, apparently, No. (*Wyrd Sisters*)

5 King, and indeed God, Teppicymon XXVII. (*Pyramids*)

6 William Scrope of Lancre. The gods probably enjoyed the irony of his dying that way while out hunting an endangered species. It takes a god to laugh heartily at this kind of thing. (*Lords and Ladies*)

7 Private Dervi Ichlos of Omnia, killed by Sergeant Simony as he dutifully aimed his crossbow at the fleeing Didactylos. (*Small Gods*)

8 Archchancellor Mustrum Ridcully's uncle, Ridcully Senior (no known forename). (*Reaper Man*)

9 The big, bad and deeply unwilling wolf in Lily Weatherwax's command performance of 'Little Red Riding Hood'. (*Witches Abroad*)

10 Zebbo Mooty, Thief Third Class, who never got the chance to boast about the privilege of being the first person to see the great Ankh-Morpork dragon. (*Guards! Guards!*)

Faculty of
CITIES AND GUILDS

The guilds of Ankh-Morpork are an integral part of
city life and (in the case of the Assassins) city death
as well. Test your civic awareness here . . .

1 It's not much fun if you're a piccolo player.

2 Represents a large profession which clearly inspires awe,
   since everyone crosses to the other side of the street when
   certain guild members walk by.

3 A guild recently outlawed by the Patrician after many
   complaints about its habit of coming round to houses and
   commenting on their unsafe status.

4 Of the various, wildly unsynchronized bells that strike noon
   in Ankh-Morpork, this guild's begins first.

5 Constable Carrot's first arrest.

6 A few of its more daring members had experimented with
   worshipping the obvious deity, in the deepest cellars of
   Guild HQ – and within a week had all died of penury,
   murder or just Death.

7 Wanted 300 dollars for a 12-course civic banquet.

8 *Nil mortifi, sine lucre.*

9 It had big red doors and official custody of the key to an
   important warehouse.

10 About once a month, it exploded.

Faculty of Cities and Guilds
ANSWERS

1 Or, indeed, a trombonist. The Guild of Musicians' punishment for a person found playing without a licence is to take their instrument and shove it somewhere tactfully unspecified. (*Soul Music*)

2 The Guild of Plumbers and Dunnikindivers, the latter being intimately involved with cesspits. (*Pyramids*)

3 The Guild of Fire Fighters had had its ways of persuading people to purchase contracts: 'Very inflammable looking place this . . . probably go up like a firework with just one carelessly dropped match, know what I mean?' (*Guards! Guards!*)

4 The Teachers' Guild – in response to the universal, heartfelt prayers of its members. (*Men at Arms*)

5 Urdo van Pew, arrested for being President of the Guild of Thieves, Burglars and Allied Trades. Which is an unthinkable charge on which to arrest anybody – 'Like a common criminal!' (*Guards! Guards!*)

6 The Gamblers' Guild thus learned the unwisdom of worshipping the Lady, the Goddess Who Must Not Be Named, who only comes when not called. (*The Colour of Magic*)

7 The Master of the Fellowship of Beggars found it necessary to beg for things like this or a 16-bedroom mansion for the night, as being more appropriate to his status than, for example, half a dollar for a cup of tea. (*Guards! Guards!*)

8 'No killing without payment' – the sacred maxim of the Assassins' Guild. Assassins are also expected to give a receipt. (*Pyramids*)

9   The Butchers' Guild, whose doors were kicked in
    during Lance-Constable Cuddy's search for the Pork
    Futures Warehouse key. (*Men at Arms*)

10 The Alchemists' Guild headquarters. You could almost
    set your calendar by it.

Faculty of
RADIOPHONICS

In this examination you will be presented with a series of small wooden boxes containing sound effects magically trapped in wires. Listen carefully to each and identify its origin.

1 *Whauauauaummmmm-eeeee-gngngn.*

2 OOOOeeeOOOeeeOOOeee.

3 OoooOOOOooooboffooo-OOOooo.

4 GrooOOowwonnogghrhhooOOo.

5 *KKKkkkkkkhhheeee . . . kkkhheeeeeee . . . keeee . . . ee . . . ee . . . ee . . . ops.*

6 *wipwipwip.*

7 Hnufhnufhnufblort.

8 *glong-glong-glong.*

9 ICE, Ice, ice.

10 *glink.*

11 Aaaaerrrrscream-gristle-gristle-gristle-crack.

12 Whumm . . . whumm . . . whumm . . . whumm . . . whumm . . . whumm . . . whummwhumm*whumm*WHUMM. *Plib.*

175

ANSWERS

1 A chord played by Buddy of the Band With Rocks In, on his primal guitar – at the Hide Park Free Festival, but you're not required to identify it *that* closely. (*Soul Music*)

2 Only half a mark if you didn't add the mental note that the wails of Mr Ixolite the banshee in *Reaper Man* are not *sounds* . . . Owing to a speech impediment he writes them down and pushes them terrifyingly under your door.

3 Windle (Undead) Poons attempting to be fearsome at a gang of muggers. (*Reaper Man*)

4 Ruby the voluptuous lady troll's night-club song about, literally, experiencing the pleasant feeling of being hit over the head with a rock by Chondrodite, the troll god of love. (*Moving Pictures*) Not a million miles, when translated, from Marlene Dietrich's performance in *Blue Angel*: 'Vunce again I am fallink in luf, / Vy iss it I now am a blue colour?', etc.

5 The ultra-high-pitched but descending sound of the Djel pyramids as they cease to flare at dawn. (*Pyramids*)

6 Menacing noise of a red-hot film can whizzing through the air immediately after the detonation of the *Odium* cinema. (*Moving Pictures*)

7 The magic-shop proprietor in *The Light Fantastic* demonstrating the offensive laugh that earned him his terrible fate.

8 The noise of an empty beer bottle being bounced along cobblestones – when hauled by a skeletal rat. (*Soul Music*)

9 The sinister echo in the octagonal tunnels of the Temple of Bel-Shamharoth, after Twoflower has remarked that he can hear the gods' dice.* (*The Colour of Magic*)

10 The sound of Carrot's bedsprings when energetic things are happening above them, usually involving Lance-Constable Angua. (*Men at Arms*)

11 Last noises heard from Mr Hong after he opened the Three Jolly Luck Take-Away Fish Bar on the site of the old temple in Dagon Street on the night of the winter solstice when there also happened to be a full moon. (*Men at Arms, Soul Music*)

12 The resograph registering a relatively minor disturbance in the fabric of reality. (*Moving Pictures*)

* On Discworld, Einstein could never have got away with saying, 'The Gods do not play dice.' A lightning bolt would have corrected him half-way – if the appropriate fire god managed to roll a double six.

Faculty of
CONTINUUM
ONTOLOGY IV

One last time: Complete or continue these sequences, as indicated by the blanks.

1 War, Terror, Panic, ——.

2 Small Bat, ——, Hunting Cloud, Fat Cows, Three Bright Stallions.

3 I Meant It For The Best, I Thought You'd Like It, For The Sake Of The Children, ——.

4 Making an Affray, Riotous Behaviour, Obstructing an Officer of the Watch in the Execution of his Duty, Assault with a Deadly Weapon, ——.

5 Altar dusting, temple cleaning, sacrificial stone scrubbing, ——, hassock repairing.

6 Piper, ——, Leaper.

7 Sniffles, Chesty, Nostril, ——.

8 Lord of the Horizon, Keeper of the Way, the Flail of Mercy, the High-Born One, ——.

9 Paperclips, shirt packaging pins, radiator keys, marbles, bits of crayon, ——.

10 Hong, Sung, Tang, McSweeney, ——.

ANSWERS

1 Clancy – these are the known members of the War family, with sons Terror and Panic and young daughter Clancy.* (*Interesting Times*)

2 Anticipated Monkey – the list is of the various years which it can simultaneously be according to local calendars over about 100 square miles of Discworld. (*Wyrd Sisters*)

3 We Are Equal Opportunity Employers – the last of the good intentions in big stone letters which, as Rincewind and Eric discover, traditionally form the stairs to Hell. (*Eric*)

4 Malicious Lingering. The reference is to Carrot's spoken charge-sheet after attending his very first Mended Drum brawl. (*Guards! Guards!*)

5 Honorary vestigial virgining is the omitted devotion forced by Mrs Cake on whatever religion's priests are currently suffering her attentions. (*Reaper Man*)

6 Drummer. The three are the named stones in the circle called the Dancers. (*Lords and Ladies*)

7 Lack of Tissues is missing from this list of the Four Horsemen of the Common Cold. (*Interesting Times*)

8 The Never-Dying King – the closing sequence of the majestic titles of the King of Djelibeybi. High Priest Dios recites the whole lot 11 times in the course of a few pages, so there is *no* excuse for forgetfulness . . . (*Pyramids*)

9 Mysterious sections of herb-chopping devices *and/or* old Kate Bush albums – all are common forms taken by continuously created matter in order to allay cosmologists' suspicions. (*Eric*)

10 Fang. These are the murderously competitive Noble Families of the Agatean Empire. (*Interesting Times*)

* Also known as Mars, Phobos, Deimos and Clancy.

Faculty of
ℙARAZOOLOGY II

More on the strange creepy creatures of Discworld
and all that surrounds it . . .

1 The popular song claims that, in order to take this animal
   aback, you need to stand on a stool.

2 The clocks these build to nest in (as part of a courtship
   ritual) would impress naturalists more if they didn't keep
   such rotten time.

3 They look like a cross between a soft-shelled crab and an
   industrial vacuum cleaner.

4 A relativistic beast, roughly leopard-sized, which moves so
   rapidly that, if you can see it, it's already somewhere else.

5 Used in a brief attempt by Granny Weatherwax to thrash a
   disrespectful alligator.

6 A group of them is known as a *slump* or an *embarrassment*.

7 It clung grimly to the ceiling rather than let itself be
   plunged into a pot of boiling water. (Wouldn't you?)

8 It magically arrived at 500mph and proved to be 20 feet
   across, one inch thick and deep fried.

9 A very large animal with the cloistered living habits of a
   soft-shelled crustacean.

10 Also known as the Lappet-Faced Worrier, it is a
   prerogative of queens.

Faculty of Parazoology II
ANSWERS

1 The giraffe. Nanny Ogg sings: '. . . with a giraffe, / If you stand on a stool, / But the hedgehog can never be buggered at all.' (*Wyrd Sisters*).

2 A variety of cuckoo native to the Ramtops. (*Reaper Man*)

3 The evolved fish, or pifcine population, which are able to live in the River Ankh. They tend to explode in fresh water. (*Soul Music*)

4 The Ambiguous Puzuma. (*Pyramids*)

5 The species of snake known as a Three-Banded Coit. It considered biting her nose, but thought better of it. (*Witches Abroad*)

6 Swamp dragons. (*Guards! Guards!*)

7 The squid intended as part of a special Brindisian meal at the Opera House: in terror it gripped the sides of the pot and sprang straight up into the air . . . (*Maskerade*)

8 A kangaroo from the continent of XXXX, which had encountered the sharp end of a teleportation-related triangle of velocities. (*Interesting Times*)

9 The hermit elephant of Howondaland, like the hermit crab, lacks a thick skin . . . so it lives in huts. Herds of these shy creatures resemble small villages moving across the plains. (*Men at Arms*)

10 The wowhawk – presumably like a goshawk, but less so – is what the Lancre rules of falconry allow queens to fly. It is small and shortsighted, prefers to walk everywhere, and faints at the sight of blood. (*Lords and Ladies*)

Faculty of
'VEGETOLOGY

Vegetables, herbs, flora, all those things so famous
for being full of quiet fun . . .

1   A herb that is sovereign against fluxes of the bladder.

2   Invoked as an occasional nickname for the Discworld's
    greatest city, mainly because it is very much an acquired
    taste which many will run for miles rather than risk
    acquiring.

3   The enchanted Horn of Furgle was wont to blow all by
    itself when in the presence of danger or of this.

4   When it's brown, explained Fruntkin the short-order chef,
    that means it's ripe.

5   Their effects include giant purple singing slugs, talking
    pillars of flame and exploding giraffes.

6   One of these unintended vegetables still thought it was a
    stoat.

7   Ingredient in experimental zombie formula #94, along
    with Red Stripefish liver.

8   A species of geranium, according to the *Dictionary of
    Eye-Watering Words*.

9   Principal flora, export, and fauna diet of the Sto Plains.

10 It met an untimely end at the age of 31,734, cutting short
    an interesting 17-year conversation.

Faculty of Vegetology
ANSWERS

1   Five-leaved False Mandrake, according to Magrat. (*Wyrd Sisters*)

2   The wahooni or wahoonie, noted for smelling terrible, growing 20 feet long, and being covered in spikes coloured like earwax. Thus, in the tradition of the Big Apple, Ankh-Morpork is known to some as the Big Wahooni. (*Moving Pictures*)

3   Horseradish. (*Soul Music*)

4   Celery. Well, what did you expect at Borgle's commissary? (*Moving Pictures*)

5   The red mushrooms with yellow spots which grow in the desert after the annual rains. St Ungulant has analysed the situation closely and suspects that the giant purple singing slugs, etc., are attracted by the mushrooms. He is right. (*Small Gods*)

6 Pumpkins, resulting from Magrat's early experiments with the fairy-godmother wand. In striking contrast, her later experiments tended to yield *more* pumpkins. (*Witches Abroad*)

7 Maniac root. It didn't work. (*Reaper Man*)

8 Funes. Hence the well known Ankh-Morporkian phrase, 'It had him by the funes.' (*Guards! Guards!*)

9 Cabbages. But travel far enough and you may find the cabbage fields excitingly varied with a few beans. This is generally regarded as the high-point of any Sto Plains journey. (*Soul Music*)

10 The oldest of the Counting Pines, which, in hope of preventing human beings from cutting them down to count their rings, display their age on the trunk – here 31,734. This tree was cut down for the benefit of the front gates of Nos. 31, 7 and 34 Elm Street, Ankh-Morpork.* (*Reaper Man*)

* One bonus mark for sheer pedantry if you argued that the 17-year duration of the conversation following the mention of the tree's number seems to indicate that the lucky houses should have been numbers 31, 7 and 51.

Faculty of
PARAPSYCHOLOGY II

More of those questions designed to make your grey
matter spurt in twin streams from your ears . . .

1 What species of whisper is unsuited to a desert environment?

2 Similarly, why in Omnia is it unsuitable for even a
rapacious merchant to make both ends meet?

3 What was the cross-eyed gorgon's recurring problem?

4 'You can't get it out of the carpets, you know. Not even
with vinegar.' What *is* this disgusting by-product of
spiritualism?

5 Whose counting system didn't go as far as three but went
'one . . . many. Many times'?

6 What, left out all night in the mountain regions of Syrrit,
would often be found next morning *facing the other way* –
without the apparent intervention of any human agency?

7 What sort of person sits down and *writes* a maniacal laugh?

8 What was incorrectly identified as 'Surprised Hedgehog' or
'Rabid Stoat'?

9 Who, according to the *Farmer's Almanac and Seed
Catalogue*, inflicted an extremely fishy fate on 14 unnamed
persons?

10 What's another term for 'Sort of bendy educational thing'?

Faculty of Parapsychology II
ANSWERS

1 Hoarse whispers. In arid Djelibeybi, camel whispers are employed instead. Ships, likewise, are 'camels of the sea'. (*Pyramids*)

2 In even more arid Omnia, meat is less indulged in by the desert folk. Hence Cut-Me-Own-Hand-Off Dhblah prefers to make both ends hummus.* (*Small Gods*)

3 She kept turning her own nose to stone. (*Guards! Guards!*)

4 Ectoplasm – the Mrs Cake viewpoint. (*Reaper Man*)

5 Rabbits in general – specifically 'Mr Thumpy'** in *Moving Pictures*.

6 Sheep. Some phenomena must remain for ever inexplicable by puny human mentalities. (*Reaper Man*)

7 The Opera Ghost, or so it would appear. Multiple exclamation marks were featured!! Which – a recurring Discworld insight – are a sign of madness!!! Or of wearing one's underclothes on one's head!!!! Or even both!!!!! (*Maskerade*)

8 Victor Tugelbend's uncle's hand shadow-play representation of 'Lord Henry Skipps and His Men beating the Trolls at the Battle of Pseudopolis'. (*Moving Pictures*) If you remembered this as, say, 'Lord Herman Scoggs and His Men beating the Dwarfs at the Battle of Psephopolis', we suppose you can have the mark you were going to give yourself anyway.

9 '14 die at hands of Chume, the Notorious Herring Thrower.' (*Reaper Man*)

10 A learning curve. (*Guards! Guards!*)

---

* In the Agatean Empire of *Interesting Times*, it rains cats and food.

** Who resented this christening and tended more towards 'Not-Mr-Thumpy', 'Call-me-Mr-Thumpy-and-die', etc.

Faculty of
UNNATURAL
HISTORY

Concerning the doings of the differently alive . . .

1   The logical part-time occupation for a retired ghoul.

2   On hearing that his heart was in the right place, he was dismally aware of the exact shelf.

3   Zombie partner of Lady Sybil Ramkin's man of business.

4   In life his eyes had appeared to others as eight-faceted and eerily insectile, which may or may not have helped break the ice at parties.

5   A last resting-place from which vampires have never been able to rise.

6   Notoriously had eyes like that dwarf who runs the delicatessen on Cable Street.

7   An endangered species last heard of in Skund.

8   Helped a lady upstairs with her luggage, but she had to help him upstairs with his arms afterwards.

9   Undertook a determined course of fitness exercises, progressing painfully from dust motes to sand grains and even whole dried peas.

10 Was intensely aggrieved by the difficulties of building one's own crypt out of cheap two-by-four from Chalky the Troll's Wholesale Building Supplies.

Faculty of Unnatural History
ANSWERS

1 Children's party catering, carried out by old Mrs Drull since her retirement. (*Men at Arms*)

2 The late King Teppicymon XXVII, glumly watching the embalmers at work: his heart was in jar three on the top shelf. (*Pyramids*)

3 Mr Slant of Morecombe, Slant & Honeyplace. Morecombe (Lady Sybil's family solicitor) and Honeyplace are vampires. Promotion prospects in this firm are poor since dead men's shoes are still occupied. (*Guards! Guards!* and *Maskerade*)

4 Greicha of the Wyrmberg, a 15th-grade wizard who had been poisoned three months earlier by his daughter Liessa but stayed around, 'in an unofficial capacity', to annoy all three of his children. (*The Colour of Magic*)

5 Greebo's digestive system. 'Vampires have risen from the dead, the grave and the crypt, but have never managed it from the cat.' (*Witches Abroad*)

6 That is, eyes like gimlets . . . Windle Poons in his new rôle as zombie. (*Reaper Man*)

7 The Five-Headed Vampire Goat of Skund, which was seriously endangered by the barbarian Truckle. (*Interesting Times*)

8 Reg Shoe, militant zombie and founder of the Fresh Start Club for life-challenged minorities ('You Don't Have To Take This Lying Down!'). (*Men at Arms*)

9 The late King Verence of Lancre, the most muscular ghost recorded in the Discworld chronicles. (*Wyrd Sisters*)

10 Count Notfaroutoe, alias Arthur Winkings – formerly a coming man in the wholesale fruit and vegetable business, now a reluctant vampire. (*Reaper Man*)

Faculty of FREGOLOGY

All these clues to Discworld items and concepts
will yield up their secrets once you spot the
common key.

1   Damnable circles.

2   Great black feline.

3   Ichor.

4   Orders.

5   Ritual requirement.

6   Counterw.

7   Origami seal.

8   Turtles.

9   Spectral visions.

10   Magic darn.

ANSWERS

The common key is a number, as hinted by 'Fregology' – of course *you* knew that the mathematician Gottlob Frege gave a classic definition of number in 1879.* *(Pause while much rotted vegetation flies at the setter of this paper.)* As for the actual number: which other one could it possibly be?

1 There are Eight Circles in Discworld's Hell, with a fine view of all eight from Pandemonium city. (*Eric*)

2 Eight plus panther gives Captain Eightpanther, that well known brand-name for travelling provisions from the Agatean Empire. (*The Colour of Magic*)

3 Eight is the number of the ichor god Bel-Shamharoth. It is a traditional hilarious quip among wizards that you shouldn't say it out loud or you will be ate alive. (*The Colour of Magic*)

4 Eight orders of wizardry** are recognized in the Unseen University hierarchy. (*The Light Fantastic*)

5 Eight wizards are needed to perform the Rite of AshkEnte.

6 Add 'eight' for Counterweight, name of a well known continent.

7 The Eightfold Seal of Stasis.

8 Eight new turtles are hatched when Great A'Tuin approaches the red star. (*The Light Fantastic*)

9 Eight colours in the Discworld spectrum: the usual seven plus octarine, which is the Colour of Magic.

10 Eight plus iron gives – no, not a golf club. A needle of octiron, as well as pointing infallibly to the Discworld's Hub, will also miraculously darn socks.

* 'The number of things in a given class is the class of all classes that are similar to the given class.'

** Including the Illuminated Mages of the Unbroken Circle, reminding us that the Unbroken Circle is one of many weird cults featured in the *Illuminatus!* trilogy (1975) by Robert Shea and Robert Anton Wilson.

Faculty of
PHILOSOPHY

Which of the Discworld's many intrepid
philosophers and other Great Thinkers did as
follows?

1   Got thrown through a pub door for attempting to restate
    the paradox of Epimenides the Cretan?

2   Invented a mathematics of eight-dimensional space while
    lying down with his nostrils closed in a violent
    sandstorm?

3   Propounded a famous Divisibility Paradox which was
    named after him?

4   Proved conclusively that all places are one place and that
    the distance between them is but an illusion?

5   Managed to reconcile the proof mentioned in the
    foregoing question with the many aspects of our
    existence which it failed to explain, such as signposts?

6   Used a pair of dividers to mathematically evaluate a pie?

7   Recreated an invention of Hero (or Heron) of
    Alexandria?

8   Told a long fable about a fox, a turkey, a goose and a
    wolf who had a wager to see who could stay longest
    underwater with heavy weights tied to their feet?

9   Is generally associated with a two-fingered gesture?

10 Pondered the ancient question of tinned salmon – the
    paradox that all the tins are the same size, even though
    salmon get thinner at both ends?

Faculty of Philosophy
ANSWERS

1   Ibid. Epimenides of Crete supposedly said: 'All Cretans are liars' – a statement whose truth is difficult to assess. Ibid tried to illustrate it by supposing in the pub that Xeno of Ephebe might say 'All Ephebians are liars' – which made Xeno fighting mad. (*Small Gods*)

2   Evil-Smelling Bugger, renowned as the greatest camel mathematician of all time.* (*Pyramids*)

3   Noxeuse, whose Divisibility Paradox demonstrates the impossibility of falling off a log. (*Soul Music*)

4   The massed astro-philosophers of Krull. (*The Light Fantastic*)

5   Ly Tin Wheedle saved the day by arguing that, although it was indeed true all places were one place, that one place was *very large*. (*The Light Fantastic*)

6   Pthagonal, who found the ratio of the circumference to the diameter unaesthetic. 'Three point one four one and lots of other figures. There's no end to the buggers . . . I mean, three point five, you could respect.' (*Pyramids*)

7   Urn, Didactylos's nephew and assistant, who constructed a steam engine closely resembling Hero's (Heron's) executive-toy design. But lots bigger. (*Small Gods*)

8   Iesope. Sounds suspiciously like Aesop . . . (*Pyramids*)

9   Didactylos, whose name actually means 'two fingers' or 'two-fingered'. (*Small Gods*)

10 Corporal Nobbs of the City Guard, Night Watch. Not all great thinkers have received their due recognition in Ephebe. (*Soul Music*)

---

*   And presumably dead, since the *current* greatest mathematician in the world is the camel called You Bastard.

Faculty of
CLAIRAUDIENCE IV

One last time: whose voice in each case?

1 *DO YOU WANT THIS STATE OF AFFAIRS TO CONTINUE?*

2 '   !'

3 *We detect a trick. We do not listen.*

4 The star is life, not death.

5 Now, got a sick dragon to see to. Little devil hasn't touched his tar oil for days.

6 Pog-a-grodle-fig!

7 AAaaaaeeeeeee – wizzaaardsah staaafff has a knobontheend, knobontheend –

8 Aaalwaaays waanted to bee ginger.

9 I *old* oo, ugger *ogg*!

10 I shallll go there directlly.

ANSWERS

1   The dragon in *Guards! Guards!*, intimidating Lupine Wonse.

2   Ginger in *Moving Pictures*, as Holy Wood magic gets out of hand and the world becomes a silent movie. (No marks for naming Victor, who is on the *other* side of the sparkling dialogue that runs: '   ,' . . . '   ?' . . . '   ?' . . . '   !'.)

3   The New Death being unsympathetic to the old one. (*Reaper Man*)

4   'Rincewind' earns you one mark; two marks, though, for 'The Spell from the Octavo speaking through Rincewind's mouth.' (*The Light Fantastic*)

5   Mustrum Ridcully in *Moving Pictures*.

6   Cyril the dyslexic cock, having drifted a long way from his 'Cock-A-Doodle-Doo!' script. (*Reaper Man*)

7   The beginning of Nanny Ogg's terrible singing in the bath, which can cause goats to give yoghurt instead of milk for weeks after. (*Lords and Ladies*)

8   Greebo the cat, temporarily in human form and – pay attention, this is complicated – donning a ginger cat mask to go to the ball. (*Witches Abroad*)

9   The great god Om in tortoise form, instructing a scalbie bird to bugger off while busy biting its foot. (*Small Gods*)

10 Imp y Celyn demonstrating his musical Llamedese accent. (*Soul Music*)

Faculty of
SILICOLOGY

The Silicon Anti-Defamation League has successfully pressured for Troll Studies courses to be included in the Unseen University curriculum, and they are now regularly taught in Room 3B. Hence this politically correct paper.

1   Who ambushed whom at the Battle of Koom Valley?

2   Who, with the aid of wings and green make-up, looked uncannily like a Balgrog?

3   Who learned, in his homeland of Copperhead in Lancre, about *Aaoograha hoa* ('She Who Must Be Avoided') and subsequently confronted her in Ankh-Morpork?

4   What exactly does the musical term *Ggroohauga* mean?

5   Who is the owner of the Cavern night-club and said to be a big man in that sinister troll crime syndicate, the Breccia?

6   Who was left holding up the ceiling?

7   Where is troll heaven considered to be?

8   Who was actually smaller than a dwarf, owing to having been repeatedly sat on by elephants?

9   Who was the only troll recorded to have been knocked out by a human, whom he later treated with great and unusual respect?

10 Who advertised on T-shirts?

11 Which Music With Rocks In band is mysteriously not listed in *The Discworld Companion*?

12 Who lit a fire on whose what?

Faculty of Silicology
ANSWERS

1   The treacherous dwarfs ambushed the noble trolls, of course.* (*Men at Arms*)

2   Morry, in *Moving Pictures*. His natural thespian talent was aided by general uncertainty as to what exactly a Balgrog might look like. Probably not a *lot* like Tolkien's Balrog in *The Lord of the Rings* . . .

3   Carborundum, hired as witch-bouncer by Mr Goatberger the publisher. He was unsuccessful in preventing the entry of She Who Must Be Avoided – i.e., Granny Weatherwax. (*Maskerade*)

4   'Music made from rocks.' Only half a mark for Music With Rocks In, which is different. (*Soul Music*)

5   Chrysoprase – though the spelling of his name has been known to vary (e.g., Chrysophrase). Unusually for a troll, he wears a suit and takes subtle rather than unsubtle offence at being called 'Chrys' by C.M.O.T. Dibbler. (*Soul Music*)

6   Detritus was lumbered with holding up the collapsing ceiling of the tunnel into Holy Wood Hill. This was his reward for being the toughest and stupidest troll to hand. (*Moving Pictures*)

7   Somewhere down below. Persons in heaven are regarded as looking benevolently up at those still Discworld-bound. (*Men at Arms*)

* Sometimes it is necessary to deduce the nature of the answer from the context of the paper. See also Faculty of Parvorectology (next paper).

8 Asphalt, later the all too appropriately named roadie of the Band With Rocks In. Others might have given up after being sat on by even one elephant, but show business was in Asphalt's soul. (*Soul Music*)

9 Detritus again, while employed as splatter – like a bouncer, but more force is used – at the Mended Drum. Probably only Constable Carrot would have been capable of this. (*Guards! Guards!*)

10 Chalky, the troll-of-all-trades. 'ChalKies, 12 The Scours, Thyngs Done.' (*Soul Music*)

11 Trollz. (*Soul Music*)

12 Herrena the Henna-Haired Harridan's party of mercenaries lit a camp fire on the tongue of the huge troll Old Grandad. This proved unwise. (*The Light Fantastic*)

Faculty of
ℙARVORECTOLOGY

Of course, the inauguration of Troll Studies courses led immediately to the arrival of delegations of small, bearded, angry Campaigners for Equal Heights called things like Thog Groinslasher, whose arguments included those unpleasantly notched double-headed axes. Hiho, hiho . . .

1 Who ambushed whom at the Battle of Koom Valley?

2 What do dwarfs love even more than gold?

3 To whom did one of the Silver Horde owe 50 dollars for a sword?

4 Who was thrown from a cold place through a small glazed aperture?

5 Which dwarf captained the school basketball team?

6 There are many recipes for Lancre dwarf bread, and most of them are a closely guarded secret apart from one common ingredient. What is it?

7 What was the first known all-dwarf rock band?

8 Whose last living action was to replace a rusted spring?

9 Who ran the Halls of Elven Perfume and Rouge Co. in Hobfast Street?

10 What is a less literal translation of the dwarf idiom 'All correctly beamed and propped?'

11 What is the standard excuse for making an unexpected appearance in a witch's kitchen?

12 Where is the museum containing many interesting examples of dwarf bread?

ANSWERS

1 The treacherous trolls ambushed the noble dwarfs, of course.* (*Men at Arms*)

2 Iron. This sounds implausible, but there it is. The official story is that songs about 'Gold, gold, gold, gold, gold, gold' are easier to sing than the metrical intricacy of 'Iron, iron, iron, iron, iron, iron' – and thus misleading signals are sent out. (*Lords and Ladies*) Dwarfs do not know the meaning of the word 'irony' but are fairly clear about the word 'iron'.

3 Fafa the dwarf. Boy Willie reckoned that, if he died in battle against odds of 100,000 to one, not having to pay that 50 dollars would leave him ahead of the game. (*Interesting Times*)

4 Lance-Constable Cuddy of the Watch, hurled through a window of the Pork Futures Warehouse before he could freeze to death. (*Men at Arms*)

5 Gloria Thogsdaughter . . . until an unfortunate axe incident. (*Soul Music*)

6 Gravel. The general idea is to bake a field ration which is long-lasting, easily packed and capable of disembowelling the enemy if skimmed through the air hard enough. (*Lords and Ladies*)

7 We're Certainly Dwarfs. A later rival – or the same group under a new name – was Dwarfs With Altitude. (*Soul Music*)

---

* Sometimes it is necessary to deduce the nature of the answer from the context of the paper. See also Faculty of Silicology (previous paper). But if you are a tedious pedant you may give yourself a mark in each paper for the politically unacceptable response that the Battle of Koom Valley is the only one known to history in which both sides ambushed each other. (*Men at Arms*)

8   Bjorn Hammerhock, an expert on mechanisms: he repaired the gonne, which then went off and killed him by a ricochet from his own anvil. (*Men at Arms*)

9   Grabpot Thundergust. He preferred to be reticent about this successful business while acting tough in dwarf bars. (*Wyrd Sisters*)

10   'Okay?' (*Guards! Guards!*)

11   'Following a seam.' The appearance was through Granny Weatherwax's kitchen floor. (*Witches Abroad*)

12   Whirligig Alley, off Rime Street in Ankh-Morpork. (*Men at Arms*)

Faculty of
INVISIBLE
WRITINGS II

Further things found written, printed, engraved, etc., within Discworld novels. Spot the context . . .

1 You Don't Have To Be 'Damned' To Work Here, But It Helps!!!

2 Because Everything. ??????

3 Security

4 Cutlet, hash, chop, stew, ragout, fricassee, mince, collops, souffle, dumpling, blancmange, sorbet, gruel, sausage, not to have a sausage . . .

5 Astounding Rains of Curry in Klatch, Amazing Death of the Seriph of Ee, Plague of Wasps in Howondaland.

6 . . . .
. . . .
. . . .
. . . .

7 *Also, dont tawk to me about farmhouses* . . .

8 They've Got Soles. FEEL THE NALES!

9 . . . the most prominent and powerful wizard in the entire country . . .

10 A Present From the Holy Grotto of Ossory.

ANSWERS

1 The new, dynamic placard over the door of Hell, covering up that old-fashioned stuff about *Lasciate ogni speranza* . . . (*Eric*)

2 Unseen University's computer Hex, responding to Adrian Turnipseed's typed-in question 'Why?'* (*Interesting Times*)

3 Legend on the oblong badges developed by various wizards who assaulted the Living Shopping Mall and, as it were, got absorbed into the system. (*Reaper Man*)

4 Twoflower's indiscriminately-used phrase book, food section. (*The Colour of Magic*)

5 Standard predictions, re-usable in any year, from the *Almanack* published by Mr Goatberger. (*Maskerade*)

6 Excerpt from the half-page of dots in Death's biography of Albert: even this book doesn't dare mention the threat of what the Dungeon Dimensions creatures might do to him if . . . (*Mort*)

7 Nanny Ogg's postcard home to her Jason ('et everybody') after having a farmhouse land on her head. (*Witches Abroad*)

8 T-shirt legend advertising Plugger the shoemaker. C.M.O.T. Dibbler was stunned that people would pay money to wear clothes with ads on. (*Soul Music*)

---

* Which, typed by Patrick McGoohan in an old *Prisoner* episode called 'The General', was enough to make an entire computer complex burst into photogenic flames.

9   Twoflower's impression of Rincewind as recorded in
    What I Did On My Holidays, aided by some bragging
    from Rincewind himself. Urinating dog, urinating dog.*
    (*Interesting Times*)

10 Inscription on a torturer's coffee mug in the cellar of
    the Quisition of the Church of the Great God Om.
    (*Small Gods*)

* As the Agateans might put it. If confused, see Faculty of Linguistics
(page 61).

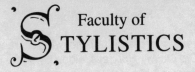

Faculty of
STYLISTICS

Concerning clothing styles and other affairs of fashion . . .

1 The most expensive perfume available in Ankh-Morpork.

2 A silk and lace confection of overpoweringly expensive tastelessness that gave its wearer the appearance of a big red jelly draped with antimacassars.

3 A functional garment that was named for its inventor.

4 The appropriate place to kit out a swordswoman so that she looks . . . exciting (leather, thighboots, etc.) . . . rather than practically dressed for her trade.

5 The sartorial utility of a sheet of cardboard under the bed.

6 What he did to his robe made it clear that he was *really* old.

7 Inserte Tabbe A into Slotte B, said the instructions.

8 The unique significance of a baggy pair of long trousers plus a long grey robe.

9 In the passing-out test of the Monks of Cool, the novice is offered all types of clothing and asked to choose this, the most stylish thing to wear.

10 Famed for wearing ultra-suave clothes in tertiary colours – the colours you get when you split blackness with an eight-sided prism.

11 They carried the vibrant message BORN TO LIVE FATS DIE YO GNU.

12 A loose-fitting brown garment of imprecise function which offered plenty of room to grow, if one planned to grow into a 19-legged elephant.

ANSWERS

1 Captivation, worn by Lady Sybil Ramkin for her successful assault upon and capture of Captain Vimes. (*Guards! Guards!*)

2 The wizard Carding's new robe, created in the proud rush of souped-up magic that followed the coming of the Sourcerer. (*Sourcery*)

3 Nanny Ogg kept calling Magrat's trousers 'Magrats', echoing Mrs Amelia Bloomer's 19th-century campaign for women's trousers (flimsy and gathered closely at the ankles), which became known as 'bloomers'. (*Witches Abroad*)

4 Woo Hun Ling's Oriental Exotica and Martial Aids, on Heroes Street, Ankh-Morpork. (*The Light Fantastic*)

5 'There's a month's soles in this,' said Captain Vimes when he found the sheet of cardboard in Filigree Street. He had a bit of a thing about making boots last. (*Men at Arms*)

6 The Bursar of Unseen University, who under the influence of Music With Rocks In took to wearing a flared robe. (*Soul Music*)

7 Magrat's Queen of Lancre outfit, including pantoffle, farthingale, ruff, and sort of things like saddlebags.* (*Lords and Ladies*)

8 The standard costume of eunuchs in the Forbidden City of Hunghung. Cohen and his invading Silver Horde were not best pleased to discover what they had been disguised as. (*Interesting Times*)

* From those fine dressmakers Boggi's of Ankh-Morpork.

9 'Hey, whatever I select.' (*Lords and Ladies*)

10 Assassins always dress in these variegated blacks, imaginable in a non-magical environment only by smoking something illegal and gazing at a starling's wing. (*Pyramids*)

11 The studs on the music-inspired leather robe made for himself by the Dean of Unseen University. (*Soul Music*)

12 'Budget clothing' bought to show off young Mort to best advantage at the Sheepridge apprentice-hiring fair. Even Death remarked, IT CERTAINLY ADDS A NEW TERROR TO POVERTY. (*Mort*)

Faculty of
TRUE NAMES II

Again, see if you can construct plausible origins for the following Discworld names . . .

1   The god Scrab.

2   The Broken Drum.

3   Movie mogul Silverfish.

4   Hoot Koomi, high priest of Khefin.

5   C.H. Lavatory & Son.

6   Red Scharron.

7   Ponce da Quirm.

8   Dark Enchantments.

9   Grope Alley, Ankh-Morpork.

10 The Dysk Theatre.

11 Corporal Cotton.

12 Mrs Scorbic.

Faculty of True Names II
ANSWERS

1 The Pusher of the Ball of the Sun is a scarab beetle, which pushes around balls of dung and was thus (to ancient Egyptians) a logical choice for the Sun's motive power. (*Pyramids*)

2 So-called because, as an alien in a non-Discworld sf novel explains, 'You can't beat it.' (*Strata*)

3 Sam Goldwyn of Metro-Goldwyn-Mayer was born Samuel Gelbfisch and called himself Goldfish for a short while before choosing the surname that became famous. Many of Goldwyn's famous remarks are echoed by Silverfish and those around him – e.g., Gaspode quotes his line about a verbal contract not being worth the paper it's printed on. (*Moving Pictures*)

4 Koot Hoomi (Sanskrit *kuthumi*, 'teacher') was one of the alleged Hidden Masters of Theosophy who fed astral knowledge to Madame Helena Blavatsky, co-founder of the Theosophical Society. Or possibly she just made him up. (*Pyramids*)

5 Bathroom suites emblazoned C.H. Lavatory & Son remind us of Thomas Crapper, who in Victorian days improved the design of flush toilets and became a big name in that field – if he wasn't one to begin with. (*Soul Music*)

6 Probably a relative of the minor sword-and-sorcery heroine Red Sonja, created by Robert E. Howard of Conan fame. (*Eric*)

7 Ponce de Leon, a Spanish grandee of our real world's 15th century, had a similar quest for the Fountain of Youth . . . (*Eric*)

8 Black Magic chocolates. But the book deviously

208

confuses the issue by also referencing the (British) Milk Tray chocolates ad: 'To deliver a box of chocolates like this, dark strangers drop from chairlifts and abseil down buildings.' (*Reaper Man*)

9 'The origin of Grope Alley's name was fortunately lost in the celebrated mists of time . . .' The same goes for the dark, disreputable alleys and lanes all over mediaeval England which were forthrightly named Gropecuntelane or something very similar. Later on there were tasteful renamings: examples are Grape Lane in York, Grove Street in Oxford, Gropelane in Peterborough, and the Grope Lanes in Bristol, Chipping Barnet and Worcester. Untrue urban folklore claims that the vanished Gropecuntelane in London was a prostitutes' hang-out but became Threadneedle Street, home of the Bank of England. Which makes you wonder about the universal Discworld euphemism of 'seamstress' for a lady of negotiable affection . . . (*Men at Arms*)

10 An obvious homage to the old Globe in London, which used to put on plays by that chap Shakespeare. 'All the Disc it is but an Theater,' wrote Hwel, 'Ane alle men and wymmen are but Players. Except Those who selle popcorn.' (*Wyrd Sisters*)

11 Corporal Cotton? Corporal Medium? Corporal Hand Wash Only? A lingering uncertainty shrouds the true names of those who have successfully Joined The Klatchian Foreign Legion To Forget, and are reduced to looking hopefully for nametags sewn into their shirts. Carry on, Legionary Size 15 . . . (*Soul Music*)

12 The Lancre castle cook who can't be having with salad and suchlike foreign muck – 'everyone knows raw vegetables are bad for you' – is named for a chemical found in raw fruit and vegetables: ascorbic acid, or vitamin C. (*Lords and Ladies*)

Faculty of
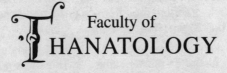HANATOLOGY

Unless your mind is moribund, these deadly
questions shouldn't be terminally difficult . . .

1 What was the problem with the traditional skeletal horse?

2 What had Mr Pounder in common with Mr Clete?

3 Why was the party expected to go downhill very quickly
at midnight?

4 What would our ancestors be thinking if they were alive
today?

5 What was the objection to the traditional symbolic chess-
game?

6 What was the scythe's final sharpening?

7 What is the reported colour of the Infinite?

8 Which singer's life ended with a final, exquisitely sung
line about 'cutting my own throat'?

9 What were the words that caused – for the very first time
– hesitation and stage fright?

10 Who, by common agreement, called him Mr Scrub?

11 What was his token in the symbolic game of Exclusive
Possession?

12 Which burden did the Ultimate Reality – whose STEED HAS
CARRIED CITIES. YEA, HE HATH CARRIED ALL THINGS IN THEIR
DUE TIME – draw the line at?

Faculty of Thanatology
ANSWERS

1 Death had grown impatient with the bother of having to stop all the time to wire bits back on. (*Mort*)

2 Both were collected by the Death of Rats rather than Death himself. (*Maskerade*, *Soul Music*)

3 That's when they thought Death would be taking off the mask he wasn't, in fact, wearing. (*The Light Fantastic*)

4 'Why is it so dark in here?' (*Pyramids*)

5 Death could never remember exactly how the knight was supposed to move. (*Sourcery*) He's still uncertain about it in *Small Gods*.

6 After beginning with a normal grindstone, oilstone and steel, following by finer sharpenings with hessian, calico, linen, satin, silk and cobweb, Death gave the scythe its penultimate edge against the dawn breeze and finished the job with sunlight. (*Reaper Man*)

7 Blue, as Death told the holy man whose preferred way to focus on the Infinite was to shut his eyes. (*Soul Music*)

8 The swan persuaded by Death to sing, '*Schneide meinen eigenen Hals –* ' or, roughly, 'I cut my own throat.' This was its swan song. Significantly for discologists, it's the Pedlar's Song from *Lohenshaak*. (*Maskerade*).

9 Death's first speech in Hwel's commissioned play *A Night of Kings*. No need to have remembered this *exactly*, but it goes 'Cower now, brief mortals, for I am Death, / 'Gainst whom no lock will hold nor fasten'd portal bar, / Here to take my tally on this Night of Kings.' In his unpractised rôle as the Grim Understudy, Death never got beyond 'bar'.* (*Wyrd Sisters*)

10 The street people of Ankh-Morpork – Foul Ole Ron, Coffin Henry, Arnold Sideways, the Duck Man, etc. (*Soul Music*)

11 The boot. It is possible that Exclusive Possession may be a little bit like Monopoly. (*Reaper Man*)

12 YOU THREE – being War, Pestilence and Famine, after their own horses had been nicked on the way to the Apocralypse. (*Sourcery*)

* He may have corpsed a little at this point.

Faculty of MUSICOLOGY

This is in fact the Hints and Cribs section. The Faculty of Musicology tuition is given by an external lecturer: Ankh-Morpork's noted entrepreneur C.M.O.T. Dibbler, who, though slightly hazy regarding rhythm and melody, knows absolutely everything about being on the fiddle.

NOTE: Many individual-question hints take the form of relevant Discworld book titles, abbreviated as follows: *The Colour of Magic* TCOM, *The Light Fantastic* TLF, *Equal Rites* ER, *Mort* Mo, *Sourcery* S, *Wyrd Sisters* WS, *Pyramids* P, *Guards! Guards!* GG, *Eric* E, *Moving Pictures* MP, *Reaper Man* RM, *Witches Abroad* WA, *Small Gods* SG, *Lords and Ladies* LL, *Men at Arms* MAA, *Soul Music* SM, *Interesting Times* IT, *Maskerade* Ma, *The Discworld Companion* TDC. Other items like short stories, Mapps and Terry Pratchett's non-Discworld works are invoked only rarely. There are, thankfully, no questions which rely on Discworld computer games.

Acronymics (pg 63) 1 towel; 2 demonology; 3 Agnes; 4 Poe; 5 Usenet; 6 morphic twin; 7 TLF; 8 WA; 9 cobbers; 10 map; 11 band; 12 see 6.

Adhesive Ultimates (pg 30) 1 IT; 2 MP; 3 TLF; 4 MAA; 5 SM; 6 MP; 7 SG; 8 Ma; 10 WS. Victims: Aliss, Lettice, Hong, Murune, Saveloy, a seamstress, Spold, a Thing, Vincent, Vorbis, yeti.

Adhesive Ultimates II (pg 170) 1 S; 2 E; 3 WA; 4 WS; 5 P; 6 LL; 7 SG; 8 RM; 9 WA; 10 GG. Victims: da Quirm, Fox, Ichlos, Mooty the thief, Peavey, Ridcully sr, Scrope, Teppicymon, Whemper, a wolf.

Ancillary Personages (pg 23) 1 TLF; 2 TCOM; 3 Mo; 4 ER;
  5 WS; 6 GG; 7 Ma; 8 E; 9 SM; 10 Mo.
Ancillary Personages II (pg 165) 1 WA; 2 SM; 3 IT; 4 Ma; 5 MP;
  6 P; 7 LL; 8 E; 9 S; 10 MAA.
Cities and Guilds (pg 172) 1 SM; 2 P; 3 GG; 4 MAA; 5 GG;
  6 TCOM; 7 GG; 8 P; 9 MAA; 10 MP, etc.
Clairaudience (pg 38) mostly Death-related, though none of the
  words in Death's HOLLOW CAPITALS are in fact spoken by Death
  himself. 1 RM, etc.; 2 Mo; 3 TCOM; 4 Mo; 5 WS; 6 Mo; 7 SM;
  9 SM; 10 Mo. Speakers other than Death: Albert, Clete, Death
  of Rats, a doorknocker, Mort, Old Tom, Scrofula, Susan,
  Tomjon.
Clairaudience II (pg 71) 1 RM; 2 S; 3 short story; 4 S; 5 non-
  Discworld novel; 6 TCOM; 7 graphic novel; 8 SG; 9 ER;
  10 MAA. Speakers: Azrael, Death x 3, the Gonne, Ipslore, the
  Lady, Om, Pestilence, Things.
Clairaudience III (pg 95) 1 Ma; 2 LL; 3 MAA; 4 TLF; 5 Mo; 6 ER;
  7 S; 8 LL; 9 MP; 10 Mo. Speakers: Agnes, Cohen, Cornice-
  overlooking-Broadway, Granny, a Hat, Osric (?), Pilgarlic,
  Ridcully, Shawn, Ysabell.
Clairaudience IV (pg 193) 1 GG; 2 MP; 3 RM; 4 TLF; 5 MP;
  6 RM; 7 LL; 8 WA; 9 SG; 10 SM. Speakers: Cyril, dragon,
  Ginger, Greebo, Nanny, New Death, Om, Ridcully, Rincewind/
  Spell, y Celyn.
Colophonics (pg 138) 1 MP; 2 MAA; 3 ER; 4 SG; 5 Ma; 6 IT;
  7 GG; 8 IT; 9 P; 10 Ma; 11 SG; 12 MAA. Speakers: ancestors,
  Beano, Billet, Fri'it, Hammerhock, Hong, Mooty, Pounder,
  Ribobe, Vorbis, Saveloy, Undershaft.
Continuum Ontology (pg 69) 1 Magrat; 2 Brethren; 3 novels;
  4 sons; 5 lifetime; 6 cards; 7 legislation; 8 fish; 9 S; 10 magic
  shop.
Continuum Ontology II (pg 91) 1 P; 2 zodiacal influence; 3 toil and
  trouble; 4 translations; 5 institutions; 6 spell; 7 vampire;
  8 chimerical; 9 Rincewind; 10 Teppic.
Continuum Ontology III (pg 119) 1 libraries; 2 quantum; 3 escapers;
  4 demon; 5 booty; 6 Assassins; 7 LL; 8 Lancre; 9 prophets;
  10 Watch.

Continuum Ontology IV (pg 178) 1 family in IT; 2 calendars; 3 steps; 4 charges; 5 devotions; 6 stones; 7 cold; 8 Djel titles; 9 spontaneous creation; 10 nobility.

Discography (pg 88) Discworld geographical equivalents invoked: Agatean Empire, Ephebe, Genua, Heliodeliphilodelphiboschromenos, Howondaland, Klatch, Llamedos, Tezumen Empire, Tsort.

Discography II (pg 110) the places: Al-Ybi, Brindisi, Brown Islands, Genua, Ku, Hersheba, Quirm, Slice, Sum Dim, Wyrmberg.

Egregiosity (pg 46) 1 dragons; 2 rank; 3 luggage; 4 time of death; 5 dwarfs; 6 dwarves; 7 mis-spelled; 8 bands; 9 multi-named; 10 which played?

Egregiosity II (pg 76) 1 Watchmen; 2 clubmen; 3 offworlder; 4 double names; 5 troll names; 6 speech; 7 cards; 8 magicality; 9 character; 10 dictionary.

Egregiosity III (pg 108) 1 books; 2 authors; 3 publication; 4 zodiac; 5 goats; 6 locations; 7 jewels; 8 orders; 9 elephants; 10 pharaoh equipment.

Egregiosity IV (pg 140) 1 demons; 2 poisons; 3 troll gods; 4 Johnson; 5 brothers; 6 studios; 7 books; 8 heroes; 9 Esk's skills; 10 Djel gods.

Eldritch Synchronicity (pg 51) 1 Lovecraft; 2 Hamelin; 3 Renaissance Italy; 4 infirm of purpose!; 5 explained in SM; 6 frankly, my dear . . . ; 7 .EXE; 8 walking fingers; 9 S; 10 award.

Eldritch Synchronicity II (pg 135) 1 Lankhmar; 2 Brown; 3 Chinese; 4 Rameses; 5 saint; 6 Alph; 7 Brown; 8 panic; 9 Baum; 10 reverse hill start.

Eschatology (pg 36) texts include two short stories, two map booklets, and *Strata*.

Eureka! (pg 58) 1 salamanders; 2 Leonardo; 3 elephants; 4 Ankh animalcules; 5 swamp dragon; 6 treadmill; 7 time pump analogy; 8 magic shop; 9 Harga's spare ribs; 10 mouldy bread.

Eureka! II (pg 99) 1 Granny; 2 Didactylos; 3 Rincewind; 4 Silverfish; 5 Dil the embalmer; 6 a lamp genie; 7 Dactylos; 8 Ramkin; 9 Whemper; 10 a bluffing doctor.

Existential Anomalies (pg 82) 1 TCOM; 2 LL; 3 RM; 4 TCOM graphic novel; 5 S; 6 bacon; 7 LL; 8 compare TCOM with IT; 9 character note; 10 compare P with MAA.

External Studies (pg 124) 1 JRRT; 2 yellow pages; 3 McGirt; 4 a grim one; 5 outside Discworld; 6 Cohen; 7 opera names; 8 artist; 9 memory/new sun; 10 aha.

First Causes (pg 18) two are from graphic-novel adaptations, and another is the opening line of two different books.

Fregology (pg 189) think of a Discworldish number and apply it mercilessly.

Gallimaufry (pg 13) these are supposed to be easy ones, but: 1 TLF; 2 IT; 3 Mo; 4 MP; 5 MAA; 6 IT; 7 TLF; 7a TCOM; 9 MP; 10 ER; 11 SG; 12 TCOM; 13 GG; 14 TCOM; 15 er . . .; 16 TCOM; 17 scythe; 18 TCOM/TLF; 19 MP, etc.; 20 for 'football' read 'dance'.

Gastrology (pg 56) linking theme: food. 1 MP; 2 WA; 3 S; 4 Ma; 5 yellow; 6 TCOM; 7 SM; 8 TLF; 9 IT; 10 LL.

Gastrology II (pg 101) 1 GG; 2 P; 3 GG; 4 SG; 5 MAA; 6 S; 7 MAA; 8 WS; 9 IT; 10 MP.

Gastrology III (pg 158) 1 Ma; 2 cf. bloat; 3 not dwarf *bread*; 4 the live sort is usually thought healthier, but . . .; 5 veins or holes?; 6 Librarian; 7 unwanted portion of mixed grill; 8 *squishi*; 9 WA; 10 E.

Headology (pg 161) 1 WA; 2 WS; 3 WA; 4 ER; 5 WS; 6 ER; 7 LL; 8 WA; 9 LL; 10 WA; 11 WS; 12 WA. Names: Annapple, Dismass, Garlick, Goatfounder, Gogol, Gripes, Hollow, Ogg x 2, Postalute, Weatherwax, Whemper.

Hysteron Proteron (pg 66) identify (at least approximately) the questions to which the quoted words are answers. Names of questioners: 1 Tugelbend; 2 Mort; 3 and 4 Ridcully; 5 Granny; 6 Rincewind; 7 Susan; 8 Unseen University examiner; 9 Bethan; 10 Brutha; 11 Death; 12 Terry Pratchett – who suggested this last question, so blame him.

Invisible Writings (pg 20) 1 Ma; 2 LL; 3 SM; 4 Mo; 5 LL; 6 IT; 7 S; 8 MP; 9 TLF; 10 WS.

Invisible Writings II (pg 201) 1 E; 2 IT; 3 RM; 4 TCOM; 5 Ma; 6 Mo; 7 WA; 8 SM; 9 IT; 10 SG.

Kleptophilia (pg 151) 1 summoning; 2 makings of magic horn;
   3 headgear; 4 hot stuff; 5 TCOM; 6 we're on a mission from
   Glod; 7 edited with teeth; 8 RM; 9 same as 3; 10 bang!;
   11 talking weapon; 12 entire building.

Ley Lines (pg 43) 1 Galileo; 2 Beachcomber; 3 Lang;
   4 underground river; 5 a collaborative thriller; 6 pole-sitter;
   7 peas; 8 sdrawkcab; 9 deadly cook; 10 cosmology.

Ley Lines II (pg 85) 1 phantom; 2 system variable; 3 short story;
   4 tortoise; 5 Cable Street; 6 Lancre history; 7 Death; 8
   L'Allegro; 9 Mo graphic novel; 10 pocket.

Ley Lines III (pg 153) 1 Klatch; 2 cat-stroking; 3 Hg; 4 TLF graphic
   novel only; 5 mum came and complained; 6 S; 7 word square;
   8 spell names; 9 Poons; 10 Significant . . .

Linguistics (pg 61) 1 IT; 2 GG; 3 MP; 4 RM/WA; 5 GG; 6 WA;
   7 TLF; 8 don't *say* it!; 9 attention-grabbing; 10 garden-related.

Linguistics II (pg 146) 1 Mo; 2 P; 3 TCOM; 4 ER; 5 TLF; 6 ER;
   7 P; 8 WA; 9 ER; 10 P.

Logopody (pg 127) linking theme: information in footnotes. 1 Mo;
   2 MP; 3 S; 4 TLF; 5 P; 6 S; 7 WS; 8 Mo; 9 MAA; 10 GG;
   11 Ma; 12 Mo.

Meganumerology (pg 156) 1 TLF or (alternative) MAA; 2 round
   number of millennia; 3 palindromic; 4 SG; 5 a power of two;
   6 neighbour of the beast; 7 see 2; 8 one fewer than the steps of
   the Tower of Art; 9 before the year 1000; 10 another round
   number.

Modern History (pg 73) 1 TCOM; 2 Unseen University; 3 P; 4 IT;
   5 S; 6 P; 7 SM; 8 GG; 9 WS; 10 P; 11 LL; 12 ER.

Morphic Resonance (pg 105) 1 bricks; 2 Hg; 3 drums;
   4 confectionery; 5 valley; 6 legion; 7 graffiti; 8 Bible; 9 sadism;
   10 long-running musical.

Morphic Resonance II (pg 116) 1 Hwel; 2 horn; 3 sdrawkcab;
   4 shadow; 5 Numbers; 6 constant births; 7 oar/rocks; 8 pie; 9 elf
   queen; 10 tortoises.

Musicology (pg 213) see Room 3B.

Numerology (pg 49) note that there are 12 answers since both 7 and
   7a feature. 2 MP (not something in it but something about it);
   3 IT; 4 rite; 5 S; 6 GG; 7 SG; 7a superstition; 8 LL; 9 WA;
   10 MP; 11 TDC; 12 WA.

Oook (pg 114) linking theme: books. 1 GG; 2 TLF; 3 E; 4 TLF; 5 GG; 6 Mo; 7 SG; 8 P; 9 S; 10 TLF.

Oook II (pg 144) 1 SG; 2 P; 3 MAA; 4 S; 5 SM; 6 MP; 7 LL; 8 SM; 9 MAA; 10 SG.

Parapsychology (pg 79) 1 MP; 2 sdrawkcab; 3 Mrs Cake; 4 grass; 5 spelt out in RM; 6 see I Ching; 7 apertures; 8 fluid named in ER; 9 stone; 10 TCOM.

Parapsychology II (pg 185) 1 P; 2 hummus; 3 nose; 4 RM; 5 Thumpy; 6 RM; 7 !!!!!; 8 shadow of historic battle; 9 herring; 10 GG.

Parazoology (pg 54) 1 P; 2 MAA; 3 WS; 4 GG; 5 LL; 6 RM; 7 GG; 8 WA; 9 MAA; 10 SM.

Parazoology II (pg 180) 1 WS; 2 RM; 3 SM; 4 P; 5 WA; 6 GG; 7 Ma; 8 IT; 9 MAA; 10 LL.

Parvorectology (pg 198) 1 see Silicology; 2 and 6 LL; 7 SM; 10 GG; 11 WA; 12 MAA. Other names: Bjorn, Cuddy, Fafa, Gloria, Grabpot.

Philosophy (pg 191) 1 SG; 2 P; 3 SM; 4 TLF; 5 TLF; 6 P; 7 SG; 8 P; 9 SG; 10 SM. Names: Didactylos, Evil-Smelling Bugger, Ibid, Iesope, Krull, Nobbs, Noxeuse, Pthagonal, Urn, Wheedle.

Physick (pg 40) 1 P; 2 Ma; 3 GG; 4 TCOM; 5 ER; 6 S; 7 SM; 8 WS; 9 GG; 10 TCOM; 11 MAA; 12 Mo.

Prefatory Commitment (pg 122) linking theme: Discworld book dedications, including one awkward one, the Mo graphic novel.

Primacy (pg 97) answers comprise *The Dark Side of the Sun*, ER, MAA, Mo x 2, *Strata*, TCOM x 4, TLF x 2.

Probability Analysis (pg 168) 1 Rincewind's return; 2 Discworld; 3 crocodile; 4 fire; 5 eagle transport; 6 Carrot; 7 scythe; 8 exam; 9 elves; 10 Vimes/Ramkin; 11 ghosts; 12 finding staff.

Pseudonymy (pg 93) 1 IT; 2 E; 3 Ma; 4 WA; 5 Mo; 6 GG; 7 LL; 8 E; 9 GG; 10 TLF. Names: Diamanda, Eric, Featherstone, Fingers, Granny, Luters, Mort, Nanny, Quezovercoatl, Rincewind.

Pseudonymy II (pg 133) 1 SG; 2 LL; 3 SM; 4 Ma; 5 IT; 6 Ma; 7 MAA; 8 GG; 9 WA; 10 MP. Names: Abraxas, Basilica, Beano, Cliff, Librarian, Saveloy, Weatherwax x 2, Withel, Wonse.

Quafficulture (pg 163) 1 Ma; 2 TLF; 3 S; 4 Mo; 5 Ma; 6 TCOM;
    7 SG; 8 GG; 9 TCOM; 10 S.
Radiophonics (pg 175) 1 SM; 2 RM; 3 RM; 4 MP; 5 P; 6 MP;
    7 TLF; 8 SM; 9 TCOM; 10 MAA; 11 MAA/SM; 12 MP.
    Sources: banshee, bedsprings, beer bottle, echo, film can, guitar,
    Hong, magic-shop owner, Poons, pyramids, resograph, Ruby.
Rhetorical Flora (pg 103) things described or compared: Ankh-
    Morpork, assault on city, astral flight, bodyguard, dragon, great-
    grandfather, inquisitiveness, mountains, night, senior wizard,
    thought, Unseen.
Silicology (pg 195) 1 see Parvorectology; 4 SM; 7 MAA; 11 SM.
    Other names: Asphalt, Carborundum, Chalky, Chrysoprase/
    Chrysophrase, Detritus x 2, Herrena, Morry, Old Grandad.
Speculation (pg 27) linking theme is mirrors. 1 SG; 2 MAA; 3 Mo;
    4 MAA; 5 WA; 6 SG; 7 P; 8 WA; 9 MAA; 10 IT.
Spellaeology (pg 142) 2 TCOM; 10 TLF. Other spells are named for
    these wizards. Atavarr, Eringyas, Gindle, Herpetty, Maligree,
    Pelepel, Riktor, Stacklady.
Stylistics (pg 204) 1 Ramkin; 2 Carding; 3 WA; 4 Woo Hun Ling;
    5 Vimes; 6 Bursar; 7 queen; 8 horde; 9 LL; 10 P; 11 Dean;
    12 Mort.
Synecdoche (pg 131) 1 not just; 2 offends; 3 everywhere; 4 run;
    5 his blood; 6 June 12th was quite nice; 7 Long Thin Debated
    Piece; 8 rest of the winter; 9 !!!!!; 10 curse; 11 trick; 12 slurry.
Thanatology (pg 210) 1 wire; 2 rats; 3 mask; 4 darkness; 5 b1–c3;
    6 dawn; 7 SM; 8 in German; 9 Hwel; 10 beggar; 11 footgear;
    12 horsemen.
Thaumoselection (pg 25) 1 ER; 2 SM; 3 TCOM; 4 IT; 5 S; 6 RM;
    7 TCOM; 7a MP; 9 RM; 10 TCOM; 11 ER; 12 Mo. Names:
    Ajandurah, Billet, Cheesewaller, Cutwell, Fresnel, Henchanse,
    Ipslore, Peavie, Poons, Ridcully, Rincewind, Stibbons.
Theology (pg 148) 1 vulture; 2 GG; 3 crocodile; 4 SM; 5 hunted;
    6 SG; 7 RM; 8 polar bird; 9 SM; 10 cutlery; 11 SG; 12 WA.
True Names (pg 33) 1 movie studio; 2 direction; 3 theatre tradition;
    4 Polish song; 5 obscure band; 6 learned citations; 7 naked
    dons; 8 voodoo; 9 Welsh; 10 Lancashire Witches; 11 1734
    satire; 12 rude euphemism.

True Names II (pg 207) 1 beetle; 2 unbeatable; 3 Gelbfisch;
   4 theosophy; 5 crap; 6 Howard; 7 Leon; 8 chocs; 9 euphemism;
   10 Shakespeare; 11 legion; 12 vitamin.

Unnatural History (pg 187) 1 MAA; 2 P; 3 GG/M; 4 TCOM;
   5 WA; 6 RM; 7 IT; 8 MAA; 9 WS; 10 RM. Names: Drull, goat
   of Skund, Greicha, Greebo, Notfaroutoe, Poons, Shoe, Slant,
   Teppicymon, Verence.

Vegetology (pg 182) 1 WS; 2 MP; 3 SM; 4 MP; 5 SG; 6 WA;
   7 RM; 8 GG; 9 SM; 10 RM. Featured plants: cabbages, celery,
   false mandrake, funes, horseradish, maniac root, mushrooms,
   pumpkins, pines, wahooni.

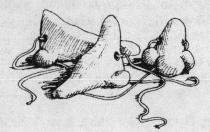

Faculty of NECESSARY IMPERFECTION

It is written that to create a perfect work of art is to usurp the omnipotence of Allah, and therefore all carpets woven by the devout contain a deliberate flaw. Just so, this devotional work avoids the wrath of the much more numerous and pugnacious Gods of Discworld by containing certain, erm, deliberate mistakes. Can you spot them?

1

2

3

4

5

6

7

8

9

10

Faculty of Necessary Imperfection

ANSWERS

Sodomy non sapiens – see page 147 for translation of this ancient and traditional academic maxim. If in fact there are any really glaring errors, you can point them out by writing to me, David Langford, c/o Gollancz or sending electronic mail to *quizbook@ansible.demon.co.uk*. Non-abusive messages may even get a reply.

*   *   *

How did you score? There are 850 basic marks to be scored, plus 10 bonus marks scattered whimsically here and there.

If you scored more than 860, you cheated. An exact 860 marks indicates precognitive talent, since one bonus-mark answer lacked a question – a career as a celebrity psychic looms for you!

Otherwise:

¶ Marks in the range 0 to 50 suggest insufficient familiarity with the Discworld saga.

¶ A score of 750 to 859 offers evidence of morbid obsession and the need to get out and about a little more.

¶ Anything in between shows that you are an utterly splendid person born under auspicious constellations, who should exercise caution in financial dealings involving persons called Dibbler, and whose lucky colour is (if I've correctly worked out the horoscope) gherkins.

*　　*　　*

The enciphered message in this book's dedication was: 'Ie, Francis Bacon, writ yt alle; give ye noe credit to that bastarde Shakspurre.'

*　　*　　*

Owing to a crippling attack of Protestant Work Ethic, I actually tried not to pinch ideas for questions from the *Companion* and *Annotated Pratchett File* . . . but used them for checking and was sobered* to find how many of 'my own' discoveries had already been spotted. Curses, foiled again. And without being told, I would certainly never have recognized that damned Polish party song . . .

On the other hand, one favourite piece of dud research for this book involved following up a widely published belief: that occasional Discworld references to sinister dogs with orange eyebrows allude to one of the countless inexplicable events recorded by Charles Fort. Allegedly a newspaper reported a dog with orange eyebrows which on 26 July 1908 said 'Good morning!' to two Pittsburgh detectives, and then disappeared in a thin, greenish vapour. Item: this story is indeed recorded in chapter 5 of Fort's book *Wild Talents*, but with no mention of the orange eyebrows. Item: even Charles Fort drew the line here – 'You can't fool me with that dog-story.'** Item: our Discworld author boggled at the supposed allusion and asked plaintively whether anyone had heard of Rottweilers. I think the conclusion must be that you can't fool us with that dog-story.

*　　*　　*

* To the point of being painfully knurd.

** He could happily swallow the 'Good morning!' but balked at the thin, greenish vapour.

Meanwhile, thanks to Terry Pratchett for writing the novels which made all this possible. Likewise to Stephen Briggs for co-writing *The Discworld Companion* and devising the maps *The Streets of Ankh-Morpork* and *The Discworld Mapp* (both drawn by Stephen Player) . . . to Leo Breebaart for the horribly voluminous *Annotated Pratchett File*, which he makes available via Internet . . . to countless frequenters of the *alt.fan.pratchett* Usenet newsgroup for their delirious inputs to the Breebaart magnum opus . . . and especially to Christopher Priest for being ever such a supportive literary agent. Also to all those feisty, wacky, zany people at Gollancz.

Earning additional grovels, Stephen Briggs offered a few theme ideas and Terry Pratchett not only pointed out ways in which I could increase my Smug Smartarse Quotient but also suggested certain questions. A competition to deduce which these are will not follow. Nor indeed has a golden turtle been buried somewhere in the Sto Plains for followers of the *hidden* clues to trace and dig up.

Goodbye . . .

David Langford, 1995

If you've just turned to the back of the book looking for the Hints section, see page 213.